Alexander H. Japp

Offering and Sacrifice

an essay in comparative customs and religious development - from the Hebrew as a starting-point to the Ritualisers

Alexander H. Japp

Offering and Sacrifice

an essay in comparative customs and religious development - from the Hebrew as a starting-point to the Ritualisers

ISBN/EAN: 9783337262594

Printed in Europe, USA, Canada, Australia, Japan

Cover: Foto ©Lupo / pixelio.de

More available books at **www.hansebooks.com**

OFFERING AND SACRIFICE

OFFERING AND SACRIFICE

AN ESSAY IN COMPARATIVE CUSTOMS AND RELIGIOUS DEVELOPMENT

From the Hebrew as a starting-point to the Ritualisers or "Catholics" in the Church of England, with significant touches all the way between

BY

A. F. SCOT, M.A.

Author of
"TALES FROM THE RABBINS AND THE KORAN," &c., &c.

LONDON
THOMAS BURLEIGH
1899

BRADBURY, AGNEW, & CO. LD., PRINTERS,
LONDON AND TONBRIDGE.

ERRATA.

1. The final ד (*daleth*) at line 6 and line 10 from bottom, p. 11, should be, of course, ר (*resh*)
2. *Waw* is at one place used for final *nun*.

ARGUMENT.

(1) Sacrifice in essentials an eating with the god. In eating, the presumption is that the spirit passes into the eater. Not only all sacrifice, but even cannibalism, is founded on this. The sacrificial animal, or substituted tree, plant, or fruit, at an early stage, was deemed to embody the soul of the deceased ancestor = god.

(2) The original of sacrifice is sharing food with ancestors. The Hebrew, מִנְחָה, very significant in relation to this. Its whole *raison d'être* is a substitution for something else. The Hebrew Scriptures distinctly recognise this. Much debate about it; but no satisfaction or consistency to be got apart from the substitutionary idea.

(3) Substitution—first, animal for human sacrifice; and then of the fruits of the earth for the animal—prevails all over, almost. Certainly it was so in the Hindu: there was first human sacrifice, then animal (especially horse) sacrifice, then the offerings of flour and ghee. But the altar itself was always so formed as to be, in the language of the "Satapatha Brâhmana," *the sacrifice is a man*. The sin-offering of the Hebrew typical as substitutionary.

(4) "The theanthropic animal" of Professor Robertson Smith universal. The Roman Catholic wafer is only the successor of a heathen wafer;

and the distinct idea that underlay it—"the unbloody sacrifice"—and that went before it, was a bloody sacrifice; it could have had no meaning whatever otherwise.

(5) One proof of what we assert is the identification of the sacrificing priest with the god, which reaches its completeness when the final stage of substitution is attained. The emblem of the god and the covering of the god become identical with those of the priest; and often the garment has a totemic character—a skin, or head, or part of an animal.

(6) Prof. Sayce, in his article on human sacrifice, says that it is unknown to the Rig-Veda. He is wrong. Prof. Eggeling is clear enough about it in the "Satapatha Brâhmana." It can be traced in every nation that derives from the early Aryans—Druids, Greeks, Danes, Germans, Celtic Britons, etc., etc.

(7) New lights thus thrown on the origin of cannibalism. Instances from many quarters. Chinese survival very noticeable. Corn-gods, etc., etc. Prof. Flinders Petrie's error about human flesh-eating, and also about the Atticottis. Witness of Red Indians, Burmans. Mr. A. Lang's inconclusive reasonings.

(8) Bearing of the word רפאים on this point; meaning of Hoama and Soma in relation to this. Roman Catholic god-eating and god-drinking simply heathen. Those who would introduce it into England are workers for Rome, and workers for a neo-paganism—nothing less. Mr. Gladstone's unfortunate position, and that of those who went with him, is from this point of view absolutely unintelligible, so long as we view them as approachably honest, intelligent Christian men.

CONTENTS.

	PAGE
ARGUMENT	V

PART I.
| Of Sacrifice Generally . | 1 |

PART II.
| Corroborative Testimony | 119 |

PART III.
| The Mazzoth or Passover . | 167 |

PART IV.
| Further Corroborations . | 181 |

| Appendices . | 217 |
| Index | 221 |

PART I.
OF SACRIFICE GENERALLY.

I.—OF SACRIFICE GENERALLY.

I.

SACRIFICE is, in essentials, an eating with the god—a sharing with him of what is pleasing to him. He is thus presumed to have tastes in common with man, to have capacities of union with him, of entering into and realising the needs of man—even physical needs of certain kinds. The anointing of sacred stones or gods-houses (Beth-els) with oil, and the pouring of libations of wine or of milk upon them, as practised by the Hebrews as well as by other nations, point decidedly in this direction.

'Sacrifice," as Grimm has right well said, "rested on the supposition that human food was agreeable to the gods,

OFFERING AND SACRIFICE.

that intercourse takes place between gods and men. The god is invited to eat his share of the sacrifice, and he really enjoys it. The motive of sacrifice is everywhere the same. . . . The human sacrifice is expiative, while animal sacrifices are simply thankofferings. The cutting off of the head, which was not consumed with the rest, but consecrated by way of eminence to the god, is significant, and points decidedly in one direction."[1]

It was only one step further to conceive of the god as in certain circumstances offering up himself or being offered, and the highest idea of offering to the savage man is, in many phases, the producing or presenting of what may be eaten! Thus, in various savage religions, we have the idea of god-eating in the most literal sense.

Most readers will remember Emerson's quaint expressions, at the opening of one of his Essays, to the effect that the first men of Guatemala ate the earth and found it

[1] "Deutsche Myth.," i. pp. 41—47.

FLESH AND SOUL IDENTIFIED.

deliciously sweet. But this needs a gloss. It was the earth conceived as a living creature, as a cow or as a bullock or a deer, with divine elements inhering in it, that they ate. They were then in the stage of predominant animism when they involved natural objects everywhere with spirit, with presences unseen and awe-inspiring, real and powerful for good or for evil to those who came near unto them.

The *rationale* of the whole observance is the identification of flesh with soul. In eating, the presumption is that the spirit passes into the eater. This, indeed, is involved in some forms of sacrifice—in all forms of totemistic sacrifice certainly. The sacred animal was presumed to embody the soul of the deceased ancestor, which had become a god. The flesh could be eaten of only after it had been consecrated—set apart. In all cases it is a holy eating—not primarily for the purpose of satisfying hunger, but for stirring the sense of association with, if not even identity with, the divine,

OFFERING AND SACRIFICE.

assumed as specially immanent in the food partaken of.

There can be no doubt whatever that the first idea of sacrificial eating lay in the offering or sharing of food with ancestors. From this custom arose the conception of a sacrificial meal, the sharing of one's food with the more generalised god, as had before been done by all the tribes to ancestors that had become tribal gods or godlings. So it was with the Jewish Jehovah, and since flesh was not everyday food with the Israelites, but a luxury, every slaughter of an animal for food was connected with sacrifice. The oldest word for sacrifice in the Hebrew is מִנְחָה, which means "gift," food offered. David Levi says the *minchah* signifies a gift or offering.[1]

Now, it is indeed very curious that this word *minchah*, which later came to mean merely a cake, originally meant an *offering*. Many attempts have been made to show how this came about. Some critics of the bolder kind say that the *minchah* was

[1] "Rites and Ceremonies," p. 192.

WHAT IS THE MINCHAH?

originally a cake made for the purpose of depositing in the little chamber near the tomb of the ancestors, and the ceremonial custom of still presenting this cake to friends or relatives is a survival from that very ancient observance. These critics point to expressions in the Hebrew indicating that the prophets protested against making such offerings to the deceased, as the Levitical law protested against their making any cuttings in their flesh, or printing marks on the body, or rounding off the corners of their hair, *for the dead;* whilst others, more conservative, say that in the *minchah* you simply have a variant of the gift of unleavened bread. One of the greatest German critics writes, "The oldest word for sacrifice in the Hebrew is *minchah*, מִנְחָה, which means gift—food offered—the sacrificial flesh being, of course, divided out and eaten."[1]

---

[1] Well may Colenso exclaim against the strange deliverance of Kuenen to the effect that no sacrifices were offered to Elohim prior to the earlier portion of Genesis. Colenso's reply is conclusive. Is it credible, he asks, that Kuenen supposed the patriarchs to have

OFFERING AND SACRIFICE.

In a note to Psalm cxli. Dr. Perowne has this: "The sacrifice here meant is strictly the offering consisting of fine flour with oil and frankincense, or of unleavened cakes mingled with oil, which was burnt upon the altar (Heb. *minchah*, English Version, ' meat-offering ') ; *see* Lev. ii. 1—21." This, however, like the "incense," was only added to the burnt-offering, the lamb which was offered every morning and evening (Ex. xxix. 38—42 ; Num. xxviii. 3—8). It would seem, therefore, that these two, the "incense" and the "offering of fine flour," &c., stand for the morning and evening sacrifices; and the sense is, "Let my daily prayer be acceptable to

offered no sacrifice at all before the delivery of the sacrificial laws of Sinai, more especially if he had before him the sacrifices mentioned in Gen. iv. 3, 4, viii. 20, 21, xxxi. 54, xlvi. 1 ; Ex. xviii. 12, and the altars built in Gen. xii. 7, 8, xiii. 4, 18, xxvi 25, xxxiii. 20, xxxv. 1—7; Ex. xvii. 15, and especially Abraham's sacrifice in Gen. xxii. 1—13, or the demand of Moses that Israel might go and sacrifice to Jahwé, Ex. iii. 18, v. 3, 8, viii. 25—28. Compare also Ex. iii. 12, x. 8, 24, xii. 31, xxii. 20, 29, 30, xxiii. 15, 18, and the words of the later history in Ex. xii. 27, " It is the sacrifice of the Pesach of Jahwé"; Ex. xix. 22, 24, " The priests that came near to Jahwé."

DR. WILLIAM MAGEE.

Thee as are the daily sacrifices of Thine own appointment." (The *minchah* is used, 1 Kings xviii. 29—36, of the whole evening sacrifice, and of the morning sacrifice, 2 Kings iii. 20.) The incense may be mentioned because, as ascending in a fragrant cloud, it was symbolical of prayer (Rev. v. 8, viii. 3—4);[1] and the same would hold also of the "meat-offering," of which it is said that the priest was to burn a part as "a memorial," a sweet savour unto Jehovah (Lev. ii. 9).

In the Hebrew *minchah nasikim*, offering of flour, flour was never offered without wine, nor wine without flour.[2]

Dr. William Magee, Archbishop of Dublin, holds that the true and original meaning of *minchah* is that of an offering presented to a superior. Thus, as he has pointed out, we find it at Gen. xxxii. 20, and xliii. 11—15, where it is used for the purpose of appeasing. Again, in

[1] The incense in a cloud-pillar was originally without doubt significant of something else.
[2] For all the different orders of *minchoth*, see what is simple and easy of access, Conder's Handbook—"Offerings," pp. 155—161.

OFFERING AND SACRIFICE.

2 Chron. xxxii. 23, and Psalm lxxii. 10, where it is applied to offerings brought by strangers to the temple at Jerusalem; and also at 1 Kings x. 25, 2 Chron. ix. 24, and 2 Kings viii. 8, 9, where it denotes gifts sent to earthly princes.[1]

The root of the word gives some further hint of the original meaning; it is מָנָה (Arabic, *manah*), to divide out, to bestow, precisely as in the giving of bread and flesh and wine, as we are told in 2 Sam. vi. 17—19, David did as well to the women as the men, after the ark had been brought in and peace-offerings had been made: "To every one a cake of bread, and a good piece of flesh, and a flagon of wine. So all the people departed every one to his house." However all that may be, it is very curious to find that the word *minchah* means both a cake, a cake for a gift, and an offering to a god or an ancestor.

Further, it is indeed remarkable that in the case of the very first offerings we have note of in the Hebrew, it is מִנְחָה לַיהוָה

[1] "Atonement and Sacrifice," ii. p. 228.

MANNA, WHAT WAS IT?

(Gen. iv. 4), something eatable—fruit from the ground brought by Cain, and a lamb by Abel. Abel brings of the firstling of his flock, and "of the fat" thereof (you see, cooked and ready for eating); and Jahwé preferred the butcher-meat to the fruits of the ground. There is no doubt of it, for the Hebrew for "of the fat" is very clear: it is מֵחֶלְבֵהֶן. I mean nothing irreverent here; I am only explicating the text and trying to show its real bearings. Jahwé was from the first clearly an eater of butcher-meat and not a vegetarian!

We find also some suggestive points in cases of the use of epithets or adjectives for substantives, *e.g.*, אָבִיר, strong (strong one), for God, the same word as is by the very same process applied to a bullock or a horse, both hailing from the same root—אָבַד, to be strong, mighty. And manna itself, most significantly, is לֶחֶם אַבִּירִים, food of the mighty. I should thank men like Principal Fairbairn and the most versatile and taste-serving Bishop of London to explain this satisfactorily on their principle.

OFFERING AND SACRIFICE.

be on our guard. It was used for premature fruit or for pasty fruit before the summer (Psa. xxviii. 4). חלב, without vowels, may be read as either milk or fat, yet when it is joined to the other word, בכרהיב, it never is used for milk, and could not so be, as Sykes well establishes. Moses never mentioned such an offering to God as milk, although it is clear that before the fall of Adam no animal was eaten, but only herbs (Gen. i. 29, 30; Gen. ix. 3). The author of the Epistle to the Hebrews says, "By faith Abel offered unto God πλείονα θυσίαν"; we render it, "a more excellent sacrifice than Cain" (Heb. xi. 4). It is rather a more ample, a more plentiful, a more copious sacrifice. But the largeness in itself was no reason why God should have regard to the one and not the other.

But this raises more difficulties than it settles. All the words for offering or sacrifice in Hebrew originally mean a gift, a present; in this respect *minchah* does not stand alone. The same thing applies

SYKES AND KENNICOTT.

to מִתָּנוּה, to תְּרוּמָה. In the latter the idea of "raising up" is very noticeable. It is from the root רוּם, to be or to become high, to exalt or to be exalted. The sacrifice by the offering itself becomes high—becomes, indeed, a part of that to which it is offered.

II.

Nothing could possibly cause me more amusement than the manner in which learned theologians close their eyes to all facts save those that suit them. Lately, that I might see how far the writings of Sykes and Kennicott, and others of that day, had really influenced English thought, I spent some time with writers like Priestley, Magee, Burgess, *et hoc genus omne*. I found it funny, before all was done. Magee, where it suited him, built on Priestley and quoted Sykes; but his great concern, on his most essential line,

OFFERING AND SACRIFICE.

was with Dr. Geddes, who wrote "Remarks on the Hebrew Scriptures," and was inclined to be rationalistic. Magee's memory of Geddes disturbed his peace, haunted him, and gave a colour to his pages. He could not get rid of Dr. Geddes, and in this fact lay Geddes' victory. Even the sense of superior influence and office did not suffice Magee. He was as though under a spell, and could not escape from it. He belabours Geddes, and yet is not content — he calls him ungentlemanly names, and yet he is not satisfied. And all that Geddes had done was to write like this :—

"But can it be believed that the whole dialogue contained in this and the following chapters is founded upon the single phenomenon of a fiery meteor or luminous appearance in a bush of briars? What may appear credible or incredible to others I know not: but I know that I can believe this sooner than I can believe that God and Moses verbally conferred together in the manner here related, on the bare

COVENANT-EATING.

authority of a Jewish historian, who lived no one can tell when or where, and who seems to have been as fond of the marvellous as any Jew of his age."

That is pretty well the received opinion nowadays, and nobody worth speaking of holds that the books of Moses were all written at one time—in the age of Moses (we beg Professor Sayce's pardon, though!) —or by one man, or even by a dozen different men![1]

The idea of food, of eating, is inextricably bound up, through all its names and phases, with sacrifice or offering. The Hebrew is most peculiar in this respect. ברית, covenant, is derived from ברר, to cut in two, to split up, to carve, to divide out; and this, again, is closely related to ברה, to eat. The custom was for the parties to any covenant to pass between the cut-up parts of the animal, as a preliminary to the sacrificing and eating together—the words כָּרַת בְּרִית, to make a

---

[1] See Cheyne's high opinion of Geddes, "Founders of Biblical Criticism."

OFFERING AND SACRIFICE.

covenant, literally being to cut up an animal, a covenant animal—or else the two words mean the same precisely; and phrases are not so formed.

בְּרִית thus undoubtedly traces from בָּרָא, to eat, to feed, which is but another form of בָּרָה, and this, again, by its infinitive, gives us בְּרוֹת and בָּרוּת, food, nourishment; so that here you have the idea of eating and cutting up flesh for eating very inextricably linked together; and the very word בָּרָא, creation, cannot but have some affinity with the foregoing, for its primary meaning undoubtedly is to cut or carve, to divide or to separate. Thus, in Hebrew, the act of sacrifice in the cutting up and dividing of the animal is creating—that is, it is feigned to produce a new element, and the idea of food and nourishment comes in next, with its own peculiar suggestions. The priest thus in sacrificing imitates the act of creation—dividing one element from another, and introducing a new one—the divine in special form and measure. At all events, by the idea of

FOOD OF MEN

feeding or nourishing at once the god and the people he is on this side also a creator or reconciler, engaged, as he believes, in making at one.

I really cannot help entertaining the idea that the לֶחֶם אֲנָשִׁים (food of men) means something very different from what the lexicographers and commentators would fain have it bear. For why, if it was a custom for friends and relatives to send food to mourners, should the prophet Ezekiel have so inveighed against it (see Ezek. xxiv. 17 and 22), any more than against simple mourning for the dead, which surely would have been unnatural and irrational? I conceive that the mourning for the dead was the feasts to ancestors, and the לֶחֶם אֲנָשִׁים the food offered to them, a portion of it eaten by the mourners. The word לֶחֶם is *often* used for feast, as it was in the allied Chaldean; and here, then, we should have the prohibition from eating the feasts of men, or of *the dead*—against which Ezekiel might well take up his parable, as here, indeed, he does.

OFFERING AND SACRIFICE.

Among the Hebrews the conception that Jehovah eats the flesh of bulls and drinks the blood of goats, against which the author of Psalm l. protests so strongly, was never eliminated from the ancient technical language of the priestly ritual, in which the sacrifices are called לחם אלהים, "the food of the deity";[1] but the word here is Elohim, which was often used for elders, judges, or ancestors. It is the word used by the witch of Endor when she speaks of "gods"—that is, ancestors (old men)—coming up.

Again: "The table of the shewbread has its closest parallel in the *lectisternia* of ancient heathenism, when a table laden with meats was set beside the idol"[2]—the idol here clearly shrining a spirit so near of kin that it could appropriate food of favourite kinds with those left behind; and, through common eating, bonds of kindredship were strengthened.

I am quite aware that in Biblical

---

[1] "Religion of the Semites," p. 224.
[2] *Ibid.*, p. 225.

BETHLEHEM.

dictionaries a wholly different meaning is given to Bethlehem, בֵּיתלֶהֶם, but I have thought much on the matter, and my conviction is that it means in origin simply the house in which offerings were made for a certain group of families to the ancestors. In many countries—say, for one, in Kafirland, or in certain parts of the hill borders of India—the chief house of a district is the temple; but in these there is no worship properly speaking, but only offerings are made to an idol which stands for the ancestors. Bethlehem—House of Bread—is, in my idea, precisely the same for the district in which it stands. Bethlehem is regarded as a translation of the older Ephratah, fruitful. This is only the other side of the same story. The ancestors, if offerings were faithfully made to them, made the place fruitful; and the passage of ancestors into gods of fertility is more easily traced than anywhere else, through the fact that faithfulness in offering to the Manes was the greatest security for fruitfulness. The

OFFERING AND SACRIFICE.

possibility of return on demonism, was marked by the slightest lapse or failure in these offerings, as seen well in the Khond among many others. By offerings: fruitfulness, welfare, success; by neglect or omission: loss, misfortune—the worshipped have asserted their original nature and become demons.

Throughout all the sacrifices of the Hebrews there thus unmistakably remained the clearest reminiscence of the offerings to ancestors just the same as elsewhere; so that it is indeed very surprising to read in the prophet's words that they actually became again what they had been in the beginning:

"Their sacrifices shall be unto them as the bread of mourners; all that eat thereof shall be polluted: for their bread for their soul [להם לנפש] shall not come into the house of the Lord." [1]

And if Jahwé, before the end, was presumed to have got above eating meat in person, yet through his priests he

---

[1] Hosea ix. 14.

MR. NESFIELD'S REMARKS.

still gorged it, and he had a power of blood-drinking still beyond all gods —he did drink it up, and by it was appeased.

The ancient rite of lustration with the sacrificial blood is said to have been the cause of inducing Jahwé to spare the Hebrew firstborn.

The sprinkling of blood and oil was originally intended to connect the priest with the deity, the blood and oil being applied first to the god or spirit resident in the stone or altar, and then to the worshippers.

In the Potraj festival the priest drinks the blood, while laymen are but permitted to eat certain parts of the flesh.

In Mr. Nesfield's account of the "Caste System of Oudh and the North-west Provinces" we have many glimpses of fine insight, and also broad and clear generalisations, which touch developments beyond his professed geographical limits. Here is an instance:

OFFERING AND SACRIFICE.

" Amongst Hindus, as amongst all other people whose religious beliefs are in the savage or barbarous state, the soul of the dead is supposed to suffer from hunger and thirst, and to need the same conveniences as it enjoyed in the body which it lately occupied."

Again :

" The object of all sacrifice in the Vedic age was to feed the gods. But as the slaying of animals to any deity except Kali is now practically extinct, the rite of feeding the gods by feeding Brahmins has succeeded to its place."[1]

Here, as elsewhere, it is true. The feast to the dead, which in every other country is eaten by the kinsmen of the departed, is in India eaten by Brahmins.[2]

Mr. Crooke tells that to the godlings of Hindu worship offerings of what is pure food to the Hindu are made—cakes of wheaten flour, and in particular those clarified by intermixture with fine butter

---

[1] Nesfield, "Caste System," p. 72.
[2] *Ibid.*, p. 71.

SACRIFICE AND FEAST.

(ghee), the most valued product of the sacred cow.[1]

Clearly, from what we have said already, the tendency in many other places, as it was among the Hebrews, is to award the tit-bits, whether of feasts to ancestors, or of feasts to gods like Jahwé, to priests, as well as the skin of the totem, or sacrificial animal, which is worn by the priests in most cases.

Thomas de Quincey, at one place in the " Posthumous Writings," has a little essay, under the title " Pagan Sacrifices," suggested by a phrase in one of the letters of Alexander the Great to his mother, in which he is led to deal with sacrifice and feasting. " With the pagans," he says, " a sacrifice to the gods universally meant a banquet to men." He who gave a banquet —a splendid public dinner—announced, in other words, that he designed to celebrate a sacrificial rite ; as, on the other hand, he who intimated a sacrifice, by the very fact

[1] " Popular Religions and Folklore of Northern India," p. 119.

OFFERING AND SACRIFICE.

proclaimed a public dinner or sacrificial feast. The suggesting lines in the letter of Alexander were concerned in inquiries of his mother about a cook; but De Quincey points out that this was not an ordinary cook, but at once a sacrificer and the preparer of a sacrificial banquet, which meant very much more. To offer up implied there, as elsewhere, an eating of portions of that offered; the offering would have had no guarantee of acceptance but for this.

To me it is almost funny to find writers like Principal Fairbairn exercising all their ingenuity to find a way of acknowledging ancestor-worship, and yet maintaining the existence of the full belief in gods long prior to it. Dr. Fairbairn, and men like him, spin shining spider-webs—oh, so neat and regular!—and then hang them up in front of them, and read the whole universe through the handy little holes in them, which makes it look so pretty, self-consistent, and explainable, according to their views. But he has to confess that "the

"AKIN TO THE DIVINE."

only notion of life outside and above nature was associated with the gods; a life akin to the Divine was attributed to the departed ancestors. Thus the belief stands enshrined in the heart of the Vedic religion, interwoven, on the one hand, with the idea of God; on the other, with the memory of the Fathers."[1]

A life *akin* to the Divine! That is good! What does *akin* mean there, and what does it include, and what does it exclude? Will Principal Fairbairn condescend to inform us why it was that alike to ancestors and to gods offerings were made of the choicest of what was edible—fruits of the earth, kidneys and fat of oxen and sheep—and why men were not to drink the blood because it was pre-eminently the gods' share — precisely what were most prized by men for their own eating—and why it was that even his own Jahwé exulted in these offerings as a savour of sweet smell, precisely as a great half-

[1] "On the Idea of Immortality," in the *Contemporary Review*, 1873.

OFFERING AND SACRIFICE.

savage warrior-king on earth might have done, with reeking shambles going on continually, as was till lately the case with human beings in Dahomey and Benin? Jahwé rejoices in hosts of offerings—holocausts—he drinks the blood of bulls and of rams, and even the shewbread, like the heathen *lectisternia*, is always there for the eating. Would Principal Fairbairn kindly say if that is not very like a great half-savage ancestor or king? It is assuredly by far more like that than a truly spiritual god such as he, looking back through his own interested Christian glasses or spider-webs, would fain make him out to be.

The mark of cleanness or fitness in the sacrifice is that it is most pleasant and agreeable to man's taste. All the Hebrew details and directions are mere attempts to hide this fact, which is ethnic.

Dionysius of Halicarnassus thus describes the sacrificial act of the Greeks: "Their hands being washed, and the victims being purified in clear water, and

THE SCAPEGOAT.

having sprinkled upon their heads the fruits of Ceres (*i.e.*, the salted meal), then having prayed, they at last ordered the proper officers to slay the sacrifice."

Washing of the hands is a mere substitute for washing of the whole body, which, indeed, was practised by the Hebrew priests at certain times and for certain sacrifices; and you have, indeed, almost the same observances among the Navajo Indians, who also had the sacred salted meal used in many ways; and among the Zunis of Arizona. "And Aaron and his sons thou shalt bring unto the door of the tabernacle of the congregation, and shalt wash them with water" (Ex. xxix. 4; Lev. viii. 6). The idea of the scapegoat is common. We find it among certain Indians, among some tribes of Africa, and among the Kafirs of the Hindu-Cush. The Egyptians were wont to deprecate evil from themselves that sacrificed, and to desire that it might fall upon the head of their sacrifice; hence they tasted not the head of any animal.

OFFERING AND SACRIFICE.

The Hebrews not only put the sins on the head of a specified animal, but they burned not the heads of certain human sacrifices, but put stones over them, or piled them up in certain places. And symbolically the idea of the scapegoat figured largely. The person who brought his sacrifice was never dispensed with from laying his hands on the head of the sacrifice.

In Fiji the priests were *tabu* from eating flesh—that is, unsacrificial flesh, as, indeed, the priests and the whole "holy nation" of the Hebrews were; all slaughtering of animals with them legally was sacrificial.

Galton tells us that no slaughter was legitimate except for sacrifice among the Damaras, the Bhagats, and many allied tribes.

The substitutionary observance, as we shall see, is exhibited in many places in the sacrifice of certain animals which are merely symbolic of the "theanthropic animal."

SACRIFICE SUBSTITUTIONARY.

III.

The idea that modified all the ancient systems of sacrifice was that of substitution and transformation by the act of consecration—the god, the priest, and the victim in the most remarkable manner interblending.

Dr. Eggeling finds this in the "Satapatha Brâhmana," first Kânda, where after dedications, etc., we read: "Now it is as an animal sacrifice that this sacrificial cake is offered." And to this sentence Dr. Eggeling gives the following note: "That is to say, the sacrificial cake is a substitute or symbol (*pratimâ*) for the animal sacrifice (as this, it would seem, was originally a substitute for the human sacrifice) by which the sacrificer redeems himself from the gods. . . . The initiation (*dîkshâ*) of the sacrificer constitutes

OFFERING AND SACRIFICE.

his consecration as the victim at the animal sacrifice."[1]

If there is no real human or divine victim, then the priest, by his putting on of hands, identifies himself at once with the god and that which is offered—he becomes part himself of the sacrifice, and thus in the mystical, but in a real sense as understood by them, he is the human sacrifice in all of bloodless that is or can be offered.

"He who is consecrated ascends to the gods," as it is laid down in the third Kânda of the "Satapatha Brâhmana"; the sacrificer being supposed to remain in an embryonic state till he has had part in the pressing of the Soma.

The Kanva text at one place reads:

"The whole earth is divine; a place of worship there is wheresoever one sacrifices on it, after enclosing it with a yagus." But the common Satapatha text is: "Verily, this whole earth is divine, on whatever part of it one may sacrifice (for

[1] Vol. i. p. 49.

SACRIFICE, FOOD OF GOD.

any one) after enclosing (and consecrating) it with sacrificial formula there is a place of worship."[1]

The officiating priests constitute the place (or medium) of worship; "wheresoever wise and learned Brâhmans versed in sacred lore perform the sacrifice, there no failure takes place; that (place of worship) we consider the nearest to the gods."

It is very characteristic that on the opening of the Fifth Kânda of the Satapatha Brâhmana, "we are told that the Asuras, thinking, 'Unto whom, forsooth, should we make offering?' went on offering into their own mouths. But the gods went on making offerings unto one another. Pragâpati gave himself up to them; thus the sacrifice became theirs: and, indeed, the sacrifice is the food of the gods."[2]

With regard to the sin-offering of the Hebrews, this substitutionary character is clear. " If he [that hath sinned] be

[1] II., p. 3.
[2] Dr. Eggeling's " Translation," vol. iii. 1.

OFFERING AND SACRIFICE.

not able to bring a lamb, then he shall bring two turtle-doves or two young pigeons, and if he be not able to bring two turtle-doves or two young pigeons, then he shall bring for his offering the tenth part of an ephah of fine flour, and the priest shall take his handful of it and burn it on the altar, according to the offerings made by fire unto the Lord."[1]

The Paschal lamb has significance only as a substitutionary victim—it stands for the human first-born, saved and devoted to God as servants. The ancient rite of lustration with the sacrificial blood is said to have been the cause of inducing Jahvè to spare the Hebrew first-born.

Prof. Robertson Smith referred to what he regarded as a very peculiar case, where a true sacrificial feast is made of the first-fruits of rice. This is called " eating the soul of the rice," so that the rice is viewed as a living creature. In such a case it is not unreasonable to say that the rice may be regarded as really an animate victim. Agricultural religions seem often to have

[1] Lev. v. 7—12.

ARABIAN MEAL-OFFERING.

borrowed ideas from the older cults of pastoral times.[1] But Prof. Robertson Smith might have gone further and fared not worse but better. This is the *raison d'être* of all substitutions for living, *i.e.*, originally human sacrifice. The Arabian meal-offering to Ocaisir is another clear and patent instance of substitution.[2]

The substitutionary character of animal offerings for human sacrifice is, in our belief, indicated in Micah (vi. 6 and 7).

"Wherewith shall I come before Jahvè, and bow myself before Elohie? Shall I come before him with burnt offerings, with calves of a year old? Will Jahvè be pleased with thousands of rams, or with ten thousands of rivers of oil? Shall I give my first-born for my transgression, the fruit of my body for the sin of my soul?"

How could first-born have been suggested here, unless under some impression of actual practice in the past?

Notwithstanding this, Mohammed in

---

[1] "Religion of the Semites," p. 242.
[2] *Ibid.*, p. 223.

OFFERING AND SACRIFICE.

the Koran, sura v., makes it the final distinction between men and gods, that the former eat food and the latter do not. Christ is only an apostle and His mother a woman, though a woman of veracity—they *both ate food*. Sale to this passage gives this note with reference to Mary. "Never pretending to partake of the divine nature, or to be the mother of God."

Here, in the absolute barring out of gods as possible eaters with man even sacrificially, you have one of the greatest advances ever made by a leader in religion—the ground is swept from beneath the feet of any possible priestly class—there is no sacrifice; Mohammedanism is the Protestant Presbyterianism of the East.

In many forms, when once the mind is awakened to it, can we trace hint and proof of this substitution. It is indeed omnipresent, and it would be painful and trying, save for the sense of progress from mere materialism to the acceptance of signs and symbols, substitutes. Thus we

THE SACRIFICIAL CAMEL.

find General Forlong writing about one particular class:—

"The various rites and sacrifices of these Bud-ā-rs used to require human victims, as noticed by Arabian travellers of the ninth century (Renaudot, p. 88), and not as now only goats, cocks, rice, fruits, and flowers."[1]

The sacrificial camel with the Arabs was expressly stated to be a substitute for a man.

At Potniæ, in Bœotia, it was the custom to kill a child as Dionysus; but in more recent times, a goat which was identified with the god, was substituted. At Tenedos a new-born calf is sacrificed to Dionysus; it was, however, shod in buskins, while the mother cow was tended like a woman in childbed, which distinctly shows it a survival of human sacrifice.

In West Africa, at Benin in New Guinea, among the Bechuanas and in many other places the same rites are practised—a human being sacrificed, cut up, and his flesh or blood used to bless the fields and

[1] "Short Studies," p. 107.

OFFERING AND SACRIFICE.

secure increase. In the Potraj ceremony of Southern India, where the goddess is worshipped as an unshapely stone stained with vermilion, an altar is erected behind the temple, oxen and sheep are sacrificed, some of them hewn in pieces and scattered right and left on the land round the village by a man who, with a large basket holding the portions, runs the circuit of the village boundaries. [May not beating the bounds with its attention to certain trees be a relic of this?]

In addition, grain was given to each of the cultivators along with a piece of the flesh still remaining, to be sown in his fields. The heads, etc., were, some of them, given to privileged persons; other portions scrambled for by pariahs, etc., who took them home with them and buried them in their land. A procession round the boundaries closed the observances—the head of the sacred buffalo is buried beside the shrine of the goddess, and then follows a perfect orgy of promiscuity, etc.

We know the legend of Hercules

THE ROMISH WAFER.

abolishing human sacrifice by substituting the figures and dress, instead of the persons of the intended victims. He persuaded the people that the gods would be equally well pleased with the shadow as with the substance. This practice of sacrificing figures instead of men continued long among the Romans. In the year 657, when En. C. Lepidus and P. Licinius Crassus were consuls, human sacrifice was abolished by decree of the senate; and clearly before that, it must have been very frequent.

Even in the wafer used by the Church of Rome in the sacrifice of the mass, which is declared to remove the sins of the people, we have two things: (1) a transference or survival of an old Pagan or Roman sacrifice, and (2), by its direct relation to that, a confession, involved even in language, that it is substitutionary, first for animal and next for human sacrifice. The little round wafer that was used in the Pagan sacrifice was called *mola*, and it was from this word that the term *immolare*, to immolate, was derived,

OFFERING AND SACRIFICE.

just, as it has been said, from *hostia* comes hostere, the one meaning to *immolate* or offer up a victim, and the other to offer up the host—the word *host* there also carrying a peculiar meaning, which directly also supports our theory here. The name later given to this wafer ceremony, which was instituted by Numa Pompilius, very significantly at once to distinguish it from the sacrifices for which it was substituted, and yet directly to connect it with them, was the " unbloody sacrifice "—precisely as was the case with the cake of flour and oil among the Hebrews. We learn too that after the *unbloody sacrifice* was ended, the image of the god was carefully taken and locked up, and then the people were dismissed with the words *missio est*—it is finished—the inferior priests, as they went out sprinkling the people with holy water that had salt in it. Now, the holy water here is a clear substitute for the blood which originally was sprinkled alike on the people and on the altar; the whole being most clearly substitutionary and no more.

THE "THEANTHROPIC ANIMAL."

The transfusion of the human into the animal is carried right down into all the forms of animal sacrifice; it remains latent and suggested though forgotten or overlooked in all sacrifices whatever. The "theanthropic animal," a phrase very happily coined by Prof. Robertson Smith, denotes the semi-divine, semi-human animal of sacrifice. On this really rests the whole conception of substitution; the "theanthropic animal" was sacrificed with a clear sense of what it was, and with the conviction that the human victim must be provided in special cases of crises or disaster, plague, defeat in arms or great losses of crops, etc., etc.

Mr. Farnell points out numberless cases of the custom in the Greek (i. pp. 94-5):—

"We can detect," he says, "in the legends, the feeling that the human victim or the divine animal is due to the God, and also the feeling that the deity himself sanctions the more merciful rite," precisely as in the Hebrew (p. 94). In the Diipolia, as in the Laphystius cult, we see that the

OFFERING AND SACRIFICE.

ideas of human and animal sacrifice are blended, precisely as in the Satapatha Brahmâna.

Here is one special point which to us has raised a great question: אֵילִים really means ram-gods; is it possible that in the ram caught in the thicket to take the place of Isaac, there is a suggestion of the God himself in his common form descending to be the sacrifice? This metamorphosis is very common in all early religions; in fact, the whole idea of sacrifice is built upon it, the consecration of the priest transforms the elements or material offering into the very God.

At Hosea xiii. 2 we find this most remarkable passage:

"And now do they add to their sin, and have made them molten images of silver, idols after their own minds, all of it work of craftsmen. They say to one another, while they sacrifice a man, let them kiss the calves."

Here, as in so many other cases, the authorized version consciously mistrans-

FOR EVERY TASTE.

lates in order to take off the onus of human sacrifice as far as it can. In the margin of reference Bibles an alternative reading to the man that sacrifices is given as "the sacrificers of man," which is nearer the original, though our version above is literal. We can make no meaning out of the last clause unless a very confirmatory one. And if the worship of the calves [=bulls] was so closely bound up with human sacrifice, as Hosea there leads us to believe it was, is it not an astonishing fact, and one that wants to be properly explained or accounted for by divinity professors and theologians and preachers, that Hosea is the only prophet of them all who explicitly and thoroughly condemns this worship of the calves! Perhaps Dr. Mandell Creighton, who, according to report, is so concerned that the Church of England, as an Established Church, should have something for every one's taste, will try to do so. Apparently many Jewish priests, prophets, and scribes were there at one with Dr. Mandell

OFFERING AND SACRIFICE.

Creighton, and thought an Established Church should have something for every one's taste, even up to or down to worship of the calves and human sacrifice. But Dr. Mandell Creighton is a man of greatest resources of taste, so he will explain it all.

The association of Moloch worship with "calf" or "ox," that is, bull-worship, is abundantly proved by the fact that in Phœnicia itself and in Carthaginia figures of Moloch have been found with an ox's head, so that probably this was the later favourite form of the god. And it may well be noted here that our modern versions which use the word "ox" in most places lead to error. The Hebrews did not castrate their cattle, and similarly their mules and their eunuchs were imported from Egypt and elsewhere. Nothing of this is hinted at about the bull in the most popular of modern books; so, for instance, the article "ox" in Smith's "Concise Dictionary of the Bible." [1]

If this is so, we can see that the

[1] "The Jew, the Gipsy, and El Islam," p. 91.

CALF WORSHIP.

Hebrews, if in this respect they did not give more than they got, certainly did in no markedly different way exhibit the tendency of that worship, so that when we read that passage from Hosea we may thus get something like a gloss upon it. "The prophets of Israel," as has been well said, "though sanctioning the calf-worship, regarded themselves and were regarded as prophets of Jehovah." When I turn to Cook's "Commentary," *ad loc.* I read: "It was Ephraim's tribal ambition which prompted him to adopt that calf-worship which paved the way at length for the worship of Baal. . . . While they slaughtered in sacrifice men, they honoured brute beasts, with the homage of adoration, reversing, as Aben Ezra observes, the proper order of things according to which they should slaughter calves and (in love) kiss men."

Old Newcome speaks to the same purport: "But at length human sacrifices were made an essential rite of the worship of calves; and this was the finishing

OFFERING AND SACRIFICE.

stroke, the last stage of the impiety that they said, let the sacrificers of men kiss the calves." The Vulgate has, "*immolate homines vitulos adorentis,*" and the Spanish version, "Los que adorais los becerros sacrificad hombres." The meaning is clear, and yet all that the English Revisers could do was to let the authorized text stand and helplessly put in the margin as reference Bibles had done already, "or *sacrificers of men.*"

Thus, while the Mosaic economy aimed at carrying forward a big scheme of substitutionary sacrifice, the Hebrews, more than any other people, were constantly aiming at going back on human sacrifice, and did it with such accompaniments of orgy, etc., etc., as render them the most patent type of relapsed savages to be found in the history of the world.

If Mr. Andrew Lang and the reader will turn to Sir R. Burton's "The Jew, The Gipsy, and El Islam," they will find at p. 11 that this daring Traveller and fine Orientalist has no hesitation about

SUBSTITUTIONARY PROCESS.

the kind of offering which Jephthah made of his daughter in fulfilment of his vow. "What nation but the Hebrew," he says, "could exult over a Jephthah 'who *did with his daughter according to his vow*,' that is, he *burnt her to death* before the Lord. He passed her over to Jahvé through the fire."[1] And surely Mr. Lang and the reader will acknowledge that Sir R. Burton knew something about that.

IV.

Thus the substitutionary process is as clearly seen in other religions as in the Hebrew or more strictly Mosaic. How much the priests' profit in all cases lay in the change, it would be hard to say; but we may be certain that if it had not been susceptible of thus being worked, it would not have been encouraged as it was. We see clearly how it did work in the Hebrew. Redemption was turned, in the first place,

[1] Page 61.

OFFERING AND SACRIFICE.

to the greatest account for temple or priestly revenue; and in the second, by it a variety of contribution was attained.

With regard to the cake of fine flour and oil, the peculiar character which it came to bear is enough. We get a light upon it from the Hindu rice and ghee cake—it was a substitute, and in that respect *represented* the first sacrifice just as well as the second, when once the view the priests took of it was understood. In both cases, the Fathers (manes) look through upon us in the whole business from the first to the last.

The Hanifa tribe of Arabs worship a lump of dough. Sale, in his preliminary discourse to translation of the Koran, says they "used it with more respect than the Papists do theirs, presuming not to eat it till they were compelled to it by famine."[1]

The Rev. Samuel M. Zwemer not long ago gave an account of the star-worshippers in a remote part of Persia. There are some very unexpected and surprising

[1] Page 16.

SYKES AND OTHERS.

elements in their cult, but their "high mystery" or communion according to Mr. Zwemer, is not so utterly inexplicable, viewed from the point of sacrifice and substitution. "On a charcoal fire some dough of barley-meal and oil are quickly baked. A deacon seizes the remaining pigeon of a pair—the other having been set free as an offering to 'the ancient light, divinely self-created'"—perhaps it has also something of the scape-goat character—"cuts its throat, and over the cakes allows four drops to fall on each in the form of a cross."

It was for lack of seeing or recognising the substitutionary element that Sykes and all the rest found it so hard to explain satisfactorily the matter of the *Minchah* and the offering of fine flour and oil. Nay more—the substitutionary character of sacrifices is realised, because the priest for the moment becomes identified with the god. Thus we have it in the case of Siva. "Siva manifested himself under eight forms, viz., ether, air, fire, water, earth, sun, moon and the *sacrificing priest.*"

OFFERING AND SACRIFICE.

Von Bohlen, Ewerbeck and Ghillany agree in finding the same corresponding substitutionary elements in circumcision—really an offering or sacrifice for another and more awful sacrifice—the smaller part for a greater part, as that greater part stood for the whole.

This idea of identification of the sacrificing priest with the god has evidence in many ways—even down to investing him with the head of the totem—as is found in Mexico, and other places. Humboldt gives a very significant drawing of a Mexican design, and says in description of it:—

"I should not have had this hideous scene engraved, were it not that the disguise of the sacrificing priest presents some remarkable and apparently not accidental resemblances with the Hindoo Ganesa [the elephant-headed god of wisdom]. The Mexicans used masks imitating the shape of the heads of the serpent, the crocodile, or the jaguar. One seems to recognise in the sacrificer's mask the

DRUIDS AND BRAHMANS.

trunk of an elephant or some pachyderm resembling it in the shape of the head, but with no upper row of incised teeth."[1]

The Druids also wrapped themselves in the skin of the animal sacrificed. We read that, thus habited, the chief Druid waited while a nobleman, with the entrails of the sacrificed animal in his hands, walked barefooted over the expiring fire thrice, to bring them to the Druid. If the nobleman escaped harmless, it was reckoned a good omen, of course, another form of survival of "passing through the fire."

When the Brâhman, the Dviga, left house and home to become an eremite in the forest, he clothed himself in a garment of bark or in the skin of the black gazelle.

The priest almost everywhere covers himself with the skin of the victim he has slain. It was goatskin in Greece and Rome, because of the association of goats with several of the Greek and Roman gods.

[1] Humboldt, Vues des Cord., pl. xv., quoted by Dr. Tylor, " Early History of Mankind," p. 304, where the plate is given.

OFFERING AND SACRIFICE.

The statue of the goat-footed deity is often to be seen in sculpture, clothed in the skin of the sacrificed goat. In Egypt the ram-headed god Ammon and his priests are found clothed with the skin of a ram.

Every scholar knows that the fawn—especially the spotted fawn—was sacred to Dionysos, and that his votaries were clad in the neblis or fawn skin.

The Brâhmans wear as a mantle the skin of the gazelle, the Kshatriyas the skin of a deer, and the Vaiçyas a goatskin.[1]

The Vajjians were the race who wore goatskins on the day of their initiation into manhood, and where priests like those of the Accadian goat-god, Uz, were clothed in goatskins.

The split fish with the head still attached on the head of Oannes as well as of his priests, is another case in point and very clear. The priest is clothed like the god, because the fish has been offered.

All the peculiar cut and colour in priests' vestments—sacrificing priests' vestments—

[1] Duncker, iv., p. 241.

SEM PRIESTS.

are, in my idea, survivals of the totem mantle, come down from far, as decidedly the bishops' mitre has reminiscences of the open fish mouth as you see it on the head of Oannes, and of his priests so long ago, yet the likeness is clear and unmistakeable. The oxen on which the Laver-sea rested in the Hebrew Temple, which, mark you, the wicked Ahaz cut down and threw out, are richly suggestive here of totemic associations.

The *sem* priest in Egypt is represented as wearing a panther's skin, and holding in his right hand a libation vase and in the left a censer, in the trial of the soul before Osiris.

Where the animal or fish was the totem, the skin or the head was that on which oath was taken; and they were the share and the covering of the priest. Indeed, in most of the old forms of oath-taking, there is some reminiscence of the totem or the sacred object associated or identified with it. In earlier times, before writing of course, there was and could have been no

OFFERING AND SACRIFICE.

sacred Book to swear on as we have; and uniformly the oath is taken on something, as we have said, accounted sacred. Thus, in Siberia, the head of a Polar bear is brought in, because the Polar bear was the totem of some of the Siberian tribes, and on that the native is sworn—the man making believe to bite it, and calling on the bear to devour him in like manner if he does not tell the truth—which really amounts to our "God strike me dead if I do not speak the truth." Among the hill tribes of India a tiger's skin is used in an exactly similar way. In New Guinea an arrow is held up by the swearer, who prays it may bring him death if he lies. Indians brandish a knife in the sunlight, and other savages swear on the sword's edge or the spear's point. The tiger's skin was used by several races or tribes, and other skins, goatskins, cowskins, etc., were used by others, this special skin being in all cases worn, or was once worn, by the priest before whom the oath is taken. The arrow is, in fact, a divining rod, and sacred

ANALOGIES.

as representing the sacred tree, and even with the Hebrews was wonder-working and holy. It was laid up in the temple in the most holy place; and each tribe was represented by its own rod—the rod of Aaron—that is, of the house of Levi, לוי, Levi = serpent, eating up all the others— the rod of the priestly caste. The knife or spear's point represents an inrush of later ideas when conquest disturbed ancient practices.

Mr. Farnell points out several analogies to this procedure with the skin of the sacrificial animal—after having treated of the ongoings of the young Romans arrayed in the skins, with strips from off them— running about on the Palatine Hill and striking women with these strips.

"It would be quite in accord with the ideas of a primitive period, when the divinity and the worshipper and the victim were all closely akin, that Athena should be clothed in the skin of her sacred animal and that ... the sacrificial skin should possess value as a magical charm. Being

OFFERING AND SACRIFICE.

used in the ritual of the war-goddess it was natural it should come to be of special potency in battle ... and it is interesting to find that the ægis in an Athenian ceremony possessed this character, being solemnly carried round the city at certain times to protect it from plague and evil, and being taken by the priestess to the houses of newly-married women, probably to procure offspring," all the children born being properly children of the state, and thus consecrated by religious observance. And what proper explanation can the Biblical critics give of Lev. vii. 8, where it is so expressly laid down that "The priest that offereth any man's burnt offering *shall have to himself the skin of the burnt offering which he hath offered*," save that this is a survival of the time when the Hebrew priest, like so many other priests, clothed himself in the skin of the offering or holy animal? But the priests in the time of David, say, made so many offerings that they would, as Colenso suggested, have been translated into fell-mongers or

SKIN OF BURNT-OFFERING.

hide-dealers, and kid and pigeon-mongers, nothing else. Were they indeed that? They were butchers of a slightly superior kind, presiding in a shambles, but fellmongers and hide-dealers wholesale, or what did they do with them? Did they heap them up as they received them till they stank? They were equal to a good deal, but surely not to this!

Now, why should the Jewish priest have had to himself the skin of the burntoffering, while the skin of the bullock offered for the sin-offering, with his flesh and his dung, should be burnt with fire without the camp? (Lev. viii. 7.) I should be glad if Dr. Fairbairn, or Dr. Clifford, or Mr. Margoliouth, or any one else, would tell me. I can imagine reasons connected with totemism and survivals of totemism to account for it, so far at all events, but instead of here venturing my own reasons, I should be glad to have theirs.

Dr. Hillier tells us that, "Among the Bantus of South Africa the dress is made of skins, but *for the chiefs the skin of the*

OFFERING AND SACRIFICE.

leopard was reserved: the skins of all other animals might be used by the people." The skin of the leopard, the totem-animal, was reserved for the chiefs, as being really high-priests, through whom the sacrifices to the totem or ancestor were duly offered, precisely as in the early days in Egypt.

We read in the Rigveda: "It is the Priest who is the Sacrifice as well as the sacrificer; so does he who is consecrated now become the sacrifice. But the sacrifice is God, and so is the Priest, and so is the man." In the Zend, the goddess Drvaçpa, to whom the ancient heroes had sacrificed, was changed into the soul of the primæval bull, which Angromainyu had slain.[1]

It is the same under more mystical conditions with Jesus Christ, who is Himself the Great High Priest, God as well as Man, and is the Sacrifice as well as the Priest. Here in the Rigveda we certainly have a suggestion of human sacrifice as being at the basis of all sacrifice.

[1] Duncker, iii., 349.

THE RIGVEDA.

Birds and animals, too, are often called to the aid of the priest; and he is the interpreter of all signs they may bring. Thus the natives of Tahiti and other Pacific Islands had a number of sacred birds and fishes which they worshipped. They imagined the god was embodied in the bird when it approached the temple to feast upon the offering. . . . The cries of these birds were regarded as the responses of the gods to the prayers of the priests.[1]

V.

Professor Sayce in his article on "Human Sacrifice among the Babylonians," published in the 4th vol. of the "Transactions of the Soc. Bib. Archæology," wrote:

"The Rigveda knows of no more costly sacrifice than that of the horse, and all our evidence tends to show that *human sacrifice*

[1] "Polynesian Researches," ii., p. 203

OFFERING AND SACRIFICE.

was utterly unknown to the primitive European Aryans." And though he admits that "it is certain that in later days human sacrifice was practised at Rome," Professor Sayce is more doubtful than in our opinion he should be, of its having been practised in early Greece. He is convinced that human sacrifice originated, not with the Phœnicians, but with the Accad-Turanians, whose idea was that God only visited the high places of the earth, and they made human offerings to him there—that the Semites learned it from them—the Semites who were so prone to learn such things from men of other races! and that contact with the early Accads accounts for the prevalence of human sacrifice in the East.[1] It is now some years since Professor Sayce published this article on human sacrifice, and I do not exactly know whether and in how far he has modified his opinions on this important subject; but there are some

---

[1] How truly remarkable! Mr. Hewitt finds that certain of the mound builders of America revived, truly revived, the high-places of the Semites.

"SATAPATHA BRÂHMANA."

facts, which, though I very deeply respect Professor Sayce and must always be grateful to him, I must here recall. First, there are abundant evidences of human sacrifices among the early Irish, the Welsh, and the early Keltic Druids, who also worshipped in groves and had holy trees. The cleft skulls which Dr. Thurnam met with in British burial mounds led him to believe that human sacrifices took place at the funeral ceremony, as with other savage races. Secondly, even if it were correct to say that "the Rigveda knows of no more costly sacrifice than that of the horse," it would still be open to point to the "Satapatha Brâhmana," and to dwell on the sentences and phrases from which Professor Eggeling draws those conclusions we have cited in favour of all sacrifices whatever, being substitutionary for human sacrifice; and thirdly, to ask whether the existence of a clear phrase for human sacrifice in the Sanskrit does not carry some weight. There are three great classes of sacrifice in the Sanskrit: (1) Asvamedha

OFFERING AND SACRIFICE.

= horse sacrifice; (2) Purushamedha = human sacrifice; and (3) Sarvamedha = sacrifice for universal rule.¹

Professor Sayce remarks that "sacrifice of Bel reminds us of the Phœnician myth" (Tennyson's poem "The Plague," would not have much foundation otherwise), which told how El—the Phœnician Bel—offered up his first-born Ye[d]ûd, the beloved [that is, David] in time of trouble by burning him on a high place, and of the parallel offered by the Biblical narrative of the sacrifice of Isaac."

In the *Asvamedha puj* the horse sacrificed is in place of the sacrificer, bears his sins with him into the wilderness into which he is turned adrift (for, from this particular instance, it would seem the sacrificial knife was not always used),

---

¹ And there can be no doubt of it—the purusha here being formed from the common पुरुष, a man. [Is not Peshawur really Purushawara = place of man-worship and therefore of human sacrifice?] Venerate, and honour the eternal masculine, Purusha, who has thousands of names, thousands of forms, thousands of heads, thousands of arms, and lives for ten thousand million years.—Hindu Hymn.

PURUSHA-PASU.

and becomes the expiatory victim of those sins.[1]

The *Purusha Sukta* of the Hindus is clearly but a spiritualised form of the Purushamedha, or human sacrifice. And if Professor Sayce had but glanced at any ordinary Sanskrit-English Dictionary he would have found the word. Purusha-pasu = man as a sacrificial victim. If there never was human sacrifice among the Sanskrit-speaking peoples, how did these words come into the language?

There can be no doubt not only of the witness but of the presence of the human sacrifice in the Satapatha Brâhmana—of the idea of substitution and the effect of consecration in making the substitutionary substance through the priest, a truly human sacrifice. Over and over again it is said: "*The sacrifice is a man.*" The altar is over and over again directed to be the size of a man, as though every other thing sacrificed must accommodate itself to that. . . .
" He who is consecrated draws nigh to the

[1] Halked, " Preface to Code of Gentoo Laws," p. 9.

OFFERING AND SACRIFICE.

gods and becomes one of the deities" (ii. 4). Once upon a time the sacrifice [human sacrifice] escaped from the gods: it became a horse and sped away from them (ii. 89). In a note at ii. p. 25, Professor Eggeling writes: "The sacrifice represents the sacrificer himself, and thus he makes sure of his offering up his entire self, and obtaining a new divine self, and a place among the immortals." At xi. 7, 13, we have: "The initiation (dîkshâ) of the sacrificer constitutes his consecration as the victim at the annual sacrifice."

But Professor Sayce might have found a still more sufficing parallel had he but turned to Mexico, and why he did not, is, we humbly confess, more than we can understand.

Phylarchus, as quoted by Porphyry, affirms that of old it was a rule with every Grecian state, before they marched against an enemy, to supplicate their gods by human victims; and, accordingly we find human sacrifices attributed to the Thebans, Corinthians, Messenians, and Temessenses, by Pausanias; to the Lace-

SACRIFICES IN GREECE.

dæmonians by Fulgentius, Theodoret and Apollodorus; and to the Athenians by Plutarch (Themis. p. 262 et Arist. p. 300, ed. Bryan), and it is notorious that the Athenians, as well as the Massillians, had a custom of sacrificing a man every year, after loading him with dreadful curses, that the wrath of the gods might fall on his head and be turned away from the rest of the citizens.[1] Here is the idea of the atonement and of the scapegoat, distinct and clear—the goat is but a substitute for the human victim.

Children were in Greece sacrificed to Chronos, or many Grecian writers speak falsely. There can be no doubt about human sacrifices as part of the worship of the Arcadian Zeus, on Mount Lycæum, or that King Lycaon offered a human child on the altar. On this matter Mr. Farnell says:

"The rite of human sacrifice on Mount Lycæum and at Alus, whatever its original significance may have been, seems to have become connected with a sense of sin and

[1] Magee, "Atonement and Sacrifice," p. 105.

OFFERING AND SACRIFICE.

the necessity for expiation; that is, with the germ of a moral idea."[1]

Did not Agamemnon sacrifice his daughter Iphigenia to turn aside the wrath of Artemis, and gain a favourable breeze for the ships of the Achæans?—this is a distinct reminiscence, if not survival of human sacrifice as propitiatory.

In Œdipus the King, we find the priest saying to the Œdipus, with reference to the relief brought by the solving of the Sphinx's riddle:

> " For thou did'st come
> And freed'st this city, named of Cadmos old,
> From the sad tribute which of yore we paid
> To that sad songstress."

And Dean Plumptre, whose fine version we have used, adds this note: " The tribute of human victims paid to the Sphinx, the nurse of the slaughtered, ' Till her riddle is solved by Œdipus.'"

Now, would Professor Sayce say that the legend of the sphinx was built on nothing; that it had not root in a reality

[1] Farnell, " Greek Cults," p. 42.

THE SPHINX.

in the far past? If so, we disagree with him; disagree with him absolutely and totally. The sphinx was merely an invention of later days to account better than otherwise could have been done for the rite of human sacrifice—better, that is, than the real facts and beliefs would have done—to put a poetic gloss on what could not be denied, other proofs being too strong, and leaving witnesses in "fossils of rite," far too evident and asserting. Through all records it is the same—the attempt is made imaginatively to account for, and to justify by other than the real reasons, the rite of human sacrifice, here among the Greeks as among other peoples.

Among the northern nations the custom universally prevailed. The Swedes even boasted of having sacrificed five kings in one day. Adam of Bremen (Hist. Eccles, cap. 234), speaking of the awful grove of Upsal, a place distinguished for the celebration of those horrid rites, says: "There was not a single tree in it that was not reverenced, as gifted with a portion of the

OFFERING AND SACRIFICE.

divinity because stained with gore, and foul with human putrefaction." Gregory the Second was obliged to make the sale of slaves for sacrifice by the German converts a capital offence; and even so late as 743, Charlemagne found it necessary to pass a law for its prevention. In face of these facts, to which many others might be added, Professor Sayce's bold statement, I confess, has proved anything but satisfactory or edifying to me; and I shall be exceedingly pleased, if he can so overthrow all these facts and statements of historians as to convince me that he is right—as I, like him, would fain look on early Aryan European history without the dreadful blot of human sacrifice than with it. Further we may quote from Mr. Borlase's "The Dolmens of Ireland."

" The rites performed by those who raised the Long Barrows of the Yorkshire Wolds were of the most barbarous kind. Limb had been separated from limb, and the bones broken" [probably that the marrow might be sucked out] "and all

IN DENMARK.

this before the tumulus had been raised over the remains. In addition to this, the human bones were accompanied by those of animals, which had been treated, apparently, in a precisely similar manner. We should not hesitate to regard the latter as evidence of feasting—what are we to say of the former?

The eminent Danish antiquary, Worsaae, has made the curious remark that in the fetich stage of the worship of ancestors, the eating of the body may have borne some direct relation to the religious ideas, which gave occasion to the feasting; and he throws out this hint to account for the discovery in the shell-mound refuse of Denmark, of disjointed fragments of the human body, and bones artificially split, just such phenomena as the Long Barrows present.

"Mr. Delgado regards the natural caves of Césaréda on the Tagus as the 'halls for cannibal feasts.' In these Spanish caves, marks of posthumous trepanning have been found, which must have been the

OFFERING AND SACRIFICE.

work of human agency, and if it be concluded that the object of making such incisions was to extract the brain, all doubt on the subject would be removed."[1]

Pliny avers, with regard to early Italian and Sicilian human sacrifices, that the difference is but small between sacrificing human beings and eating them.

Dr. Magee, building on Dr. Priestley, has it thus: "Among all heathens and especially in the time of Moses, human sacrifices were considered as most acceptable to the gods; but in the laws of Moses, nothing is mentioned with greater abhorrence, and it is expressly declared to have been a principal cause of the expulsion of the idolatrons inhabitants of Canaan. The right of the Divine being to claim such sacrifices is intimated by the command to sacrifice Isaac, but it was declined and a ram substituted in its place." Well, and Dr. Magee never so much as glances at the command of Jahvé to sacrifice a passover to him, the first-born of man and

[1] Borlase, "The Dolmens of Ireland," ii. p. 469.

DRS. SCHLIEMANN AND MANATT.

beast, and that none so devoted should be redeemed. That stands as one of the laws of Moses, and shows the patchwork.

It is even stated by the Burmans that human sacrifice is not yet unknown among the Red Karens and wild Chins and Kadus.[1]

Dr. Schliemann at Mycenæ found skeletons of men—bodies of slaves or captives immolated on the master's tomb, and deposited above the mouths of graves.[2] So in Homer, Achilles, besides holocausts of sheep and oxen, horses, dogs, etc., offers twelve valiant sons of great-hearted Trojans on the grave of his friend.

"A like usage," says Dr. Manatt, "prevailed among other people related to the Hellenic stock, and must be assumed for the Mycenæans as well."[2] We have already spoken of the human skeletons found in the *débris* about the acropolis graves, and

---

[1] Burma Census, p. 69. Human sacrifices were made up to comparatively recent times by the wild tribes of the Santal Pergunas.

[2] "The Mycenæan Age," by Dr. Christos Tsountas and J. Irving Manatt, LL.D., p 97.

OFFERING AND SACRIFICE.

not infrequently bodies are found buried in the passages of the chamber-tombs. Indeed in one of these, six entire skeletons lay crosswise before the doorway at different depths. As indications go to show that they were all buried at one time, we assume that they were slain on purpose to accompany their master to Hades, for it is certainly impossible that six slaves or captives—and such they must have been to be excluded from burial in the chamber—should have simultaneously met a natural death. The woman buried in the dromos of the Clytemnestra tomb must have been a slave, and one highly prized. . . . This pit-grave, which is without either covering or revetment, is cut directly in the dromos floor, showing that the work was done while the passage was clear. Now we can hardly believe that the dromos was closed merely for the burial of a slave, and so we infer that the woman's death was coincident with that of some one of the master's family. May we not go a step further and surmise that

AT THE LUPERCAL.

she was a favourite slain to follow her master to the underworld?[1]

Independent thinkers and good scholars have even suggested that in the human victims of the Sphinx you have a reminiscence of human sacrifices.

The truth is, this late offering up of human beings at the graves of the dead, is nothing but a survival of the offering up of human sacrifices to appease or to conciliate the earlier ancestors, who were invariably conceived as bloodthirsty and apt to avenge the slightest neglect or inattention in the severest way. Of this and allied points we shall have more to say in a later volume on "Worship of Ancestors."

Relics of human sacrifice, as is now admitted by almost all authorities, are seen in the smearing of the foreheads of the young men with the blood of the sacrifices on the Palatine at the Lupercal, and, as we have seen, a precisely similar ceremonial occurred in the somewhat similar worship of the Lycæan Zeus in Arcadia.

Ibid., p. 152.

OFFERING AND SACRIFICE.

Smearing foreheads with substitutes for blood, as with sendon and vermilion, are very common in initiation and other ceremonies of many tribes, and all point in one way.

Among the early Northmen, the number three was deemed particularly dear to Heaven, and every ninth month witnessed the groans and dying struggles of nine unfortunate victims. The fatal blow being struck, the bodies were consumed in the sacrifice, which was kept perpetually burning, while the blood, in singular conformity with the Levitical ordinances, was sprinkled, partly upon the surrounding multitude, partly upon the trees of the hallowed grove and partly upon their idols.[1]

There is, indeed, the most complete historic testimony to the fact of human sacrifice among the Celtic Druids. Here is the witness of Cæsar:—

" And for that cause such as are grievously diseased, or conversant con-

[1] Mallet, " North Antiq.," i., ch. vii.

CÆSAR AND STRABO.

tinually in the danger of war, do either sacrifice men for an oblation or vow the oblation for themselves, using in such sacrifice the ministry of the Druids, forasmuch as they are persuaded that the immortal Deity cannot be pleased but by giving the life of one man for the life of another, and to that purpose they have public sacrifices appointed."[1]

Does not Strabo, too, tell of a huge image, in the shape of a bull, of straw, into which a number of victims were packed, and then, under the priest's prayers, fire was set to it, on certain special occasions ; while Pliny adds, that they ate parts of the victim (as was indeed the imperative custom with that which was sacrificed everywhere) and the diviners divined by certain signs in the entrails? Strabo enlightens us with yet more detail about certain priestesses who stood before the Cambrian army and read auguries in the blood of their human sacrifices.

The identification of the priest with the

[1] Comm. Lib. vii. cap. ix.

OFFERING AND SACRIFICE.

sacrifice was good in conception, but it soon everywhere became the source of abuse. Human nature is weak. Men do not cease to be men because they are priests, and assumed to be at once identified with the God and the sacrifice; nay, when use and wont have made it familiar, it becomes a medium of importance and profit. What else is testified in the following Mosaic legislation?—

"What man soever there be of the house of Israel that killeth an ox, or lamb, or goat in the camp, or that killeth it out of the camp,

"And bringeth it not unto the door of the tabernacle of the congregation, to offer an offering unto the Lord before the tabernacle of the Lord, blood shall be imputed unto that man; he hath shed blood, and that man shall be cut off from among his people.

"To the end that the children of Israel may bring their sacrifices which they offer in the open field, even that they may bring them unto the door of the tabernacle of

SACRIFICE GOD-EATING.

the congregation unto the priest, and offer them for peace offerings unto the Lord."

It is laughable, nothing short of laughable, to find intelligent Christian men declare that this is the rock from which they were hewn, and to swear by such transparent priestly craft and greed and imposture as a revelation of divine truth.

All sacrifice is thus seen to be direct or more commonly indirect god-eating through the identification of the god and the priest by consecration with that which is offered, and some sacrifices are even direct god-eating, as we shall soon see.

It is not too much to say in view of all these things, that human sacrifice has its root in systematic god-making, perfected through the process of god-eating.

VI.

Indirect god-eating is thus very common. The recognition of all productiveness and fertility in nature as the work of the god

OFFERING AND SACRIFICE.

would inevitably soon lead to this. If the god is the indirect producer of all, and remains latent in it—in that which is most necessary and nourishing, and at the same time the sweetest to man's taste—then the next step is *obvious*, we eat the god; but the god is still in every portion of the same substance scattered o'er the world. The way in which the Khond sacrifice is accounted for in the fable shows all this very clearly :—

The fable runs, " that on one occasion when preparing vegetables for curry, she (Tari Pennu[1]) cut her fingers, but the blood trickling on the soil, it was immediately made fertile. On this she summoned her followers, pointing out the fruitful change, and desired that she should be cut up to complete the transformation which a few drops of the blood had effected. Her followers, who idolised her, refused to comply with her wishes,

---

[1] *Penni*, or *Pennu*, means Earth or Mother-Earth, and *taru* is the snake goddess. In Tamil, as Mr. ewitt tells, *pen*, the woman, is the Mother-Earth.

MERIAH SACRIFICE.

and, to satisfy her in a measure, they determined to purchase a victim for the purpose, and this, it is believed, originated what is termed the Meriah sacrifice."[1] Here we see very clearly the identification of the victim with the god!

The heathen Semites had all practices that looked the same way. What other significance can lie in the myth that El cut off the genitals of Baal-Samim (Lord of the Sky), and the blood flowed into the springs and streams, than that the beneficent god had imparted his life-giving, creating power to the fertilizing water, so to make earth also productive, and so to render ordinary eating veritably indirect god-eating? The prepuces cut off at circumcision festivals by the Arabs are carefully and ceremonially buried in the earth—in the fields, as assurance of plentiful seasonable rain. Clearly, we have an illustration or expression of the same idea when we read that the Roman peasants carried the Phallus across the

[1] Dr Shortt, "Trans. Ethno. Soc.," vi. p. 271.

OFFERING AND SACRIFICE.

fields to ensure their fertility. In this case, as in some others, we have the Phallus instead of parts of the human body: it was here substitutionary and representative, as it must have been in early days in many places by tribes that took oath on it.

Indeed, in the early days of the animistic stage, when water, trees, and plants were endowed with indwellers of the ghostly or divine type, how was it possible that they should escape the idea of "god-eating," even in the ordinary processes of satisfying appetite? Sacred rivers and sacred waters, to drink of which men came from far, remain even in highly-developed religions, like the Hindu, as survivals of the earlier phase, and, through partaking of them, men received a share of the divinity itself. Something of the same idea, though modified in its expression, we find running through the whole circle of heathen antiquity. The opposing nations are not only conquered, but their gods are

A CURIOUS CONFUSION.

dethroned, and if not veritably eaten, are certainly regarded as put out of court, absorbed by the gods of the conquerors.

Sir John Lubbock, treating of sacrificial eating, well remarks "that in many cases a curious confusion arises between the victim and the Deity, and the former is worshipped before it is sacrificed and eaten. Thus in ancient Egypt, Apis the victim was also regarded as the god, and Iphigenia was supposed by some to be the same as Artemis.[1]

Yet, further, in a very direct material form we have god-eating as an immediate and direct result of the worship of ancestors. The moment a grandfather or father dies he is by that very passing away deified. All that pertains to him is sacred, divine, and to be worshipped. Portions of his raiment and his hair are in many cases hung on holy trees. In many cases, too, his mortal remains do not suffer burial, or are buried temporarily and as a mere matter of form, but are burnt, and the ashes are either

[1] "Origin of Civilisation," p. 239.

OFFERING AND SACRIFICE.

mixed with bread and water, or are thrown into sacred beer or wine and drunk. Among the Tarianas and Tulchas and some other tribes of Brazil a month after the funeral, the body was disinterred and put into a great pan or oven over a slow fire till the volatile parts were driven off with the most horrible odours, leaving only a black carbonaceous mass. This was pounded to powder and mixed in several vats or conches of caxiri (native beer), which is drunk by the assembled company. They believe that thus the spirit and virtues of the deceased will be transmitted to the drinkers.[1] It was the custom of the Xomanes of Mexico to burn the bones of the dead and to mingle the ashes in their drink; for they fancied by this means they received into their own bodies the spirits of the deceased.[2] Dalton tells in the "Asiatic Society Bengal Journal,"[3] that the Birposes of India were in the

[1] Wallace, "Travels on the Amazon," p. 498.
[2] Bancroft, ii. p. 198.
[3] xxxiv. p. 118.

EATING FROM HATRED.

habit of eating their own dead and drinking their blood. They declared to him that they never shortened life to provide such feasts, and shrank with horror at the idea of any bodies save those of their own blood being served up to them. The Rajah said that he had heard of cases when an aged Bishor thought his end was approaching he himself invited his kindred to feast on his body. Purchas tells that the Venezuelans lamented their dead lords in songs; then they roasted them at a fire till almost calcined, and beating the remains to powder, drank them in wine. The Tapuyas of Brazil ate their own dead as the last demonstration of their love—the bones being reserved for marriage feasts, when they were pulverised and eaten as the most precious thing that could be offered.[1]

Eating from hatred, as among the Tatars, Aghoras, and Battaks of Borneo, springs from exactly the same idea, really to appropriate whatever of strength and

[1] Southey, i. p. 400.

OFFERING AND SACRIFICE.

skill may be in the man *eaten*. The Samoans, as we know from Dr. Turner, have no objections to eat another man's god. In Central Australia the Yulugundis even by cannibalism unite lovers parted by death, for the survivor eats the body of the departed. That is a very peculiar practice of certain classes of Burma, and suggests a very great deal, that while they are being tattooed, they must eat chunks of human flesh cut from certain parts—a thing which suggests a time when ceremonial cannibalism and tattooing absolutely went together and were indissoluble. Another noticeable point. Even where the people do not eat the flesh, or profess not to eat it, but only to cook and bury it, their doing so decidedly seems to me to point to a time when it was eaten, else why so elaborately cook it as they do? The bones are actually broken to get out the marrow. Mr. A. MacDonald clearly admits that sometimes the bodies or parts of the bodies are eaten by certain tribes which utterly disclaim any such indul-

KIDNEYS SEAT OF LIFE.

gence.[1] Certain Australian tribes denied eating the flesh, though they confess to having done it aforetimes; but now the meat was buried in the ground when roasted.

We have found from several authorities, Duncker amongst them, that "the Massagatæ (Scythians) and Derbices thought it a very miserable end to die of sickness, and killed their parents, relatives, and friends when they had grown feeble and old and ate them, preferring this to putting them in the ground and letting the worms eat them." The Cucumas of South America said exactly the same, that "it was better to be inside a friend than to be swallowed up by the cold earth." The Yamas of South America, and some other races alike in the South Pacific, and in Asia—of Burmah, in fact—suck out the marrow from the bones, in their idea thus to get the soul; while others again particularly like the kidneys, because they say the seat of life and power is there. Kidneys, in fact, even in some of the

[1] "Jour. Anthro. Inst.," ii. p. 279.

OFFERING AND SACRIFICE.

higher religions (witness the Hebrew), had a distinctly separate place as the presumed seat of life.

Captain Hinde, in his book "The Fall of the Congo Arabs," tells in a very matter-of-fact-way about the practices of certain cannibal negro tribes on the Congo, among whom pieces of human flesh are sold and bought precisely as joints of beef and mutton are amongst us. But even there there are restraints such as show glimmerings of earlier practices. Among one of the worst tribes we find that parents and near relatives could not be eaten, in this very unlike some of the cases we have given where parents, getting old, begged that they might be killed and eaten, under the idea that thus certain powers and influences passed into those who partook of their bodies. On the other hand, the Congo cannibals had scruples about this; and we read of one fellow, a black sentry, who had accidentally shot his father, but would not eat any of his corpse, but handed it over to strangers, who were not deterred

PUZZLE OF ANTHROPOLOGY.

by any such motives as were prevailing with him.

Another very peculiar point, of which we have as yet seen no sufficing explanation, is that pointed out by Peschel, who remarks that the custom is most prevalent among tribes distinguished by a certain social advance. On this point, Captain Hinde has some very quaint remarks. If the scarcity of food alone was the disposing cause of cannibalism, it should be found among the lowest in the scale—those that represent the earliest phase of development otherwise, but there can be no doubt, as Peschel says, that it is not so.

Indeed, it is one of the most remarkable puzzles of anthropology that everything tends to the conviction that cannibalism—horrible as it seems—does not originate at the early stage or become a confirmed habit till, as Hinde says, " a certain degree of intelligence, and even refinement, has first been attained."[1] And he

[1] Hinde, " The Fall of the Congo Arabs," p. 285.

OFFERING AND SACRIFICE.

then goes on to quote from Mr. Herbert Ward to the following effect :—

" It must not be supposed that the cannibal tribes of the interior are altogether brutal in every action of their life. On the contrary, I have observed more frequent traits of affection for wife and children among them than are exhibited in the conduct of domestic affairs among the people of the lower or Ba-Congo country, who are not cannibals, nor addicted to the shedding of blood, save in religious matters."[1]

The presumption, therefore, is that it does not *originate* in the fact of eating for the mere sake of eating ; but in some anterior custom or idea ; and as already said, the peculiar tribal rules about certain requirements in the method of finding the victim and dealing with it, as well as, in many cases, the summoning of certain heads and members of the tribe before the human body can be cut up into pieces, seems to favour this theory, as does also

Hinde, p. 286.

PROWESS FROM EATING.

the fact that with many human flesh-eating tribes, certain portions are absolutely the right of the priests and others of certain officials and warriors, just as under certain religions specified parts of the offerings were reserved for the priests alone, and could not be eaten by any one else.

In Captain Hinde's book we read:—
"While instances of resort to human flesh as food in times of famine are widely diffused, the most common motive seems to be the well-known superstition that by eating the heart or other part of an enemy —to which the practice is often restricted —his prowess is acquired. In Polynesia and in Central America, it occurs most frequently in connection with religious rites."

But this hardly goes far enough. What could be the origin of the idea of prowess derived from eating an enemy's flesh? Clearly it had, originally, reference to something more ceremonial, something in which the individual appeared only as represen-

OFFERING AND SACRIFICE.

tative of the tribes as we find, on looking into it, is the case in so many other similar institutions. In no such matter, when once the clan or the tribe is instituted, do men act merely as independent individuals—that is absolute. Our idea of it is that cannibalism invariably proceeds at first from tribal institution, and is really religious—it springs from the practice of human sacrifice. This is, when looked at from our point of view, confirmed by the fact that the head is not eaten by "the great majority," as Captain Hinde says—the head in sacrifice not being anywhere eaten, and this has confirmation by exceptions as proving the rule, when Captain Hinde says that "I have come across *more than one tribe* which prefers the head to any other part,"[1] which simply means that when once the *tabu* was removed by disobedience, the tabued morsel would be found specially sweet, as is usually the case when such a motive is once overcome.

Captain Fenton, speaking of the Kalangs,

[1] Hinde, p. 68

LIEUTENANT MASTER'S REPORT.

Kanôns, or Kamans, says their chief peculiarity seems to be that they eat their elderly relations when they (not the elderly relations) think they have lived long enough. "My informant said that when any man or woman became old and decrepit, their relatives assembled together, put the old person upon a high sort of bamboo scaffold, such as the Kachins erect in front of their villages in connection with their Nat-worship, and then poke them off with bamboos, so that they fall down and die; then they cut them up into small bits and cook and eat them." Lieutenant Master speaks of a tribe called Lings (? Liangs) who live in the Assam direction, north-west from the Jade Mines, who dispose of their old men and women by making them drunk, killing and eating them by boiling or, rather, cooking the flesh." This, Mr. Eales writes, requires confirmation,[1] but we regard it as very possible on our theory.

There can be little doubt that here,

[1] "Burma Census Report," Introd., p. xlv.

OFFERING AND SACRIFICE.

again, we have an instance of cannibal habits derived from the idea of strength and power and wisdom passing into the eaters, else certainly the very old and decrepit would not be indulged in only. It is the relic, really, of a religious eating, as in New Zealand.

This idea of procuring by eating the peculiar quality, mental or spiritual, of that which is eaten is very well illustrated by the anecdote of the Spartan so effectively used by the Rev. Professor Theodore Wright, in his speech at the Annual Meeting of the Palestine Exploration Fund for 1897. He said:—

"You remember the saying of the Spartan when he heard the beautiful song of the bird: 'I will catch that bird, and I will eat it, and then I shall have its voice!' And when he had plucked it and it lay in his hand, he said: 'There is nothing to eat. It was a voice and nothing more.'"

"The cannibalism of a New Zealander," says Sir John Lubbock, "was a ceremony,

UNHOLY SACRAMENT.

and not a meal; the object was something very different from mere sensual gratification: it must be regarded as a part of his religion, as a sort of unholy sacrament. This is proved by the fact that after a battle the bodies which they preferred were not those of plump young men or tender damsels, but of the most celebrated chiefs, however old and dry they might be. In fact, they believed that it was not only the material substance which they thus appropriated, but also the spirit, the ability, and the glory of him whom they devoured. The greater the number of such corpses they had eaten, the higher, they thought, would be their position in the world to come."

"Unholy sacrament!" They only did in naïfest reality what branches of the Christian Church do to-day, by the aid of the pseudo-magical expedient of transubstantiation: the one as well as the other will have it that they eat the real flesh and drink the real blood! And Lord Halifax and others address the Pope, trying to get him to say that Anglican priests can

OFFERING AND SACRIFICE.

do the same wonder of actually transforming the wine and bread into the real body and blood.

Livingstone speaks of the Manyema race as being singularly fine, physically, and of superior character, intellect, etc., yet they were confirmed cannibals.

Even with the cannibal Papuans of the Solomon Islands, no one, white or black, could be put to death for the purpose of being eaten till the whole tribe had assembled, in whose presence the rites connected with the killing were gone through, and the eating was made a feast, at which special rules held force, special parts being designed for the heads and chief men and priests of the tribe. It was certainly the case that whenever a Jew slaughtered an animal the Kohen claimed the tongue, one side of the face, and one shoulder.[1] Here we see that, even in the case of the most out-and-out cannibals we have yet come in contact with, there were some more or less clearly defined tribal rules which raised

[1] Burton's "The Jew, the Gipsy, nd El-Islam," p. 60.

GREAT DELICACIES.

the thing above a mere savage devouring of human flesh for the satisfying of hunger. The head and arm were thought to be great delicacies reserved for chiefs and kings; and so, when the chief Ysabel sent a boy's arm and hand in a present to a Spanish navigator, we need not wonder that the chief was somewhat offended and annoyed when the Spaniard declined to eat it, and ordered it to be buried. It was the most practical way the chief knew to wish the officer long life, strength, and wisdom. In confirmation we read in the *Daily Mail* of January 28th, 1889:—

VANCOUVER (B.C.) Jan. 27.

A horrible story of shipwreck and cannibalism has reached here.

The ship " Manbare," bound for Sydney, Australia, foundered off New Guinea in a hurricane, on December 11. The crew reached the shore, where they were seized by natives and hurried to a village in the interior.

There the whole tribe engaged in a wild can-

OFFERING AND SACRIFICE.

nibal orgie. Even the old women and children joined in torturing the victims, gouging out their eyes and lacerating their flesh.

Two were roasted alive. *Some were beheaded, and their heads were paraded on poles before their comrades,* who stoically watched the preparations for their own death.

One man, James Greene, escaped, and reached the coast after tramping for a day and a night without food. He was rescued by a passing steamer. The scene of horror which he had witnessed turned his hair snowy white.

Captain Guy Burrows writes: "In the practices I am about to describe, hunger is not a factor, superstition and depraved appetite the sole incentives. There is an extraordinary religious sentiment connected with this custom. The flesh of relatives is never eaten, and some tribes forbid the use of human flesh to all women." . . . But to our idea Captain Burrows somewhat inconsistently adds: "The real origin of cannibalism was hunger, and by a pro-

FLESH FORBID TO WOMEN.

cess of heredity and warlike proclivities, it grew into a cult. The most common cause seems to be the well-known superstition that by eating the heart or other part of an enemy his prowess is assimilated or acquired."

If this latter was the most common cause, then clearly the real origin of cannibalism does not in most instances, if any, lie in hunger pure and simple. "A process of heredity and warlike proclivities" would not inevitably or naturally raise a custom founded merely in brute necessity into a cult. The truth is, the idea of partaking of the flesh of an enemy to secure or appropriate his power, or strength, or wisdom, is evidenced in other than direct ways. The utter abstinence from eating the flesh of relatives, unless under religious consecration, is almost invariably found, and the forbidding the use of human flesh to all women. If the origin of eating human flesh was in any case hunger merely, why should it in such case have been forbidden to women, who are, surely, as susceptible to the pangs of hunger as men are?

OFFERING AND SACRIFICE.

The Indian of Hayti would have thought he was wanting in respect to the memory of a relative if he had not thrown into his drink a small portion of the body of the deceased after having dried it and reduced it to powder.[1] The Tupinambas of Brazil defended their practice of drying and eating the bones of their ancestors mixed with their food by saying that the soul of the dead man remained in the bones and lived again in the living.[2] In the Brahminical period in India, which succeeded to the Vedic, human sacrifice seems to have prevailed. It is even believed by many that the sects called Sāktas or Tantrikas formerly ate portions of the flesh and drank the blood of the victims sacrificed at their secret orgies.[3] Eating the fetish, as practised by many tribes, is significant too. Among the Issini and others it was a solemn ceremony, observed only when taking an oath, etc.

---

[1] Humboldt and Boupland, v. 248.
[2] Brinton, p. 258.
[3] Monier-Williams, p. 64.

KHONDS OF ORISSA.

Almost invariably the priest had to eat a part of whatever was offered. The *rationale* of human sacrifice thus indicates the fact of god-eating in the form of relics of deified ancestors. In Guatemala, for example, the bodies of those sacrificed were eaten as holy food—the hands and feet, as delicacies, being presented to the high priest and ministers at the altar. The lower forms of cannibalism we would fain account for as degenerations from this practice. At all events, the eating of human flesh and the drinking of human blood in the vast majority of cases was originally really god-eating and god-drinking—partaking of the body of the deified ancestor under the idea that the spirit would live in those who partook of the remains.

Even in the human sacrifices of the Khonds of Orissa—the victims before death being raised to a kind of divine honour—you have what is indirectly a god-eating. Certain parts of the body of the victim are cut up into small portions and sent to each district, and there planted in

OFFERING AND SACRIFICE.

the ploughed earth, so as to appease the anger of the goddess of Earth—who with them is also goddess of destruction—Tarri Pennu, that they might eat of plenteous crops, thus purchased by divine sacrifice![1]

It is all too clear that the Negro-Arab tribes, like those others mentioned, originally ate their dead—that the earlier custom was ceremonial, or based on religious ideas. The habit survives among many backward tribes still, or did recently, with probably no sense of its original significance whatever; only in connection with it very often is the reminiscence of totemistic observance —the imitation of the totem animal in movement and otherwise, when engaged in the effort to secure the cannibalistic meal. This points a long way—a very long way. This is like the tattoo marks pointing very far back, and sufficing to prove that cannibalism, like the cannibalism of the New Zealanders and tribes of the South Pacific, was not originally what it now is. All

[1] See Macpherson's " Khonds of Orissa," *passim*.

EFFENDI GIFOON'S FACTS.

this is amply confirmed by the translation which Captain Marshall has given of the life of Ali Effendi Gifoon, a member of the Shilluk tribe, in which he says:

"The Fertit tribe used in their own country to eat each other freely, and when a man was so ill as to render the chance of his recovery improbable, he was bought in advance by the highest bidder. The Fertit had no graves, and there is no word for 'graveyard' in their language. Years later, when I was serving at Amedeb, Zobeir Pasha sent down a large number of Soudanese to serve as soldiers in the Kassala district. Among them was a Fertit named Abd el Bayin, whose teeth were like fangs and were always carefully filed. This man had come straight from his own country, where, as I said before, no dead were buried, and the privation he was now required to undergo was more than he could endure. One night he rose and crept out of the lines. Finding a little boy asleep by his mother's side in a neighbouring zeriba, he seized him, and then

OFFERING AND SACRIFICE.

ran off with his prey into the plain. The child screamed loudly, and its cries roused the mother, who speedily raised an alarm. The cannibal wrung the boy's neck as he ran, and fled on until he thought he was safe from pursuit. Then he commenced his repast. The soldiers, who had been aroused by the woman's cries and lamentations, had in the meantime turned out, and, having formed a ring, gradually drew in upon him. Then Abd el Bayin, who, *after the manner of his country, had assumed the form of a hyena when he carried the child off*, rose up, and stood a soldier once more, with the mangled remains of the boy at his feet. He was at once arrested, and, after reference to Khartoum, it was decided to send him back to his country. I remember another tribe who during the winter nights used *to habitually assume the form of hyenas*, and, prowling round our Shilluk villages, would seize and devour any children they could find. These were the Kesirra, a tribe of nomad Arabs of almost white complexion, who habitually ate the

HUMAN LIVER.

corpses of human beings or animals whenever they could find them. To this day we all believe that some of the hyenas which prowl and roar at night round the villages in the Soudan are men in disguise. Many of those we used to hear around us when we were together at Tokar were really Arabs. We all can tell them from their peculiar cries. There was once a Fungowi, Mek Gahman, of Senaar, of whom it is related that, having tasted human liver, he had a child killed every day. His servant had gone to the bazaar to buy meat, and on his return homewards a kite swooped down upon the contents of the basket, which he was carrying upon his head. Alarmed by the gestures of the servant, he dropped a piece of meat which he had in his claws into the basket, but managed to secure the sheep's liver which the servant had purchased for his master. Accordingly, the meat dropped by the kite, which also proved to be liver, was in due course cooked and served up to the mek. As soon as he tasted it he pronounced the

OFFERING AND SACRIFICE.

flavour to be different from any he had yet known, and closely questioned his servant, who assured him that he had bought it as sheep's liver in the market. Being unable to believe this, he caused cattle, sheep, goats, gazelle, and all kinds of animals to be killed, in order that he might see to which kind it belonged; but all in vain. Finally it occurred to him that a human being was the only species he had not tasted; so the next time a child died he caused its liver to be cooked. Then he immediately recognised the flavour which had become so precious to him, and after this he caused a child to be killed and its liver served up to him every day. In due course his unpopularity among his subjects became so great that his brother Ismail was induced to fall upon him suddenly, and kill him."[1]

The hyena was, almost without doubt, the totem animal of these man-eating Arab tribes.

[1] "Memoirs of a Soudanese Soldier,' in the "Cornhill Magazine" for August, 1896.

BOUGHT FROM OUTSIDERS.

The Scythians esteemed cannibalism, we read, a sober and religious system.[1]

Cannibalism is known to be still preferred by some savage tribes to the expedient of using their dogs for food under pressure of famine; and the wild natives of an American coast on one occasion frankly avowed this to a European voyager, saying that "their old women were not so useful as their fox-like curs!"[2]

The human creatures sacrificed by the Khonds must be bought from outsiders. They were often procured as mere children, and kept in readiness, and many of them were not offered till they had reached man's estate. They might even marry and beget children, and the children were Meriahs also—*i.e.*, to be offered. One peculiar thing is that they were well cared for—treated, in fact, as though something of sacredness attached to them. It is notice-

---

[1] "Christian Religion's Appeal to the Bar of Reason," ii. 37, Latham.
[2] Cupples' "Deerhounds," p. 177, footnote.

OFFERING AND SACRIFICE.

able that they were made to grow long hair, which was cut off some ten or twelve days before the day fixed for sacrifice. For three days a kind of orgie is held, and on the first day and night frantic dances are indulged in, and there is much drinking. On the second morning the victim is carefully washed, dressed in a new garment, and led forth in solemn procession, with music and wild dancing. The place of sacrifice is invariably amid deep, shadowy forest groves, at some distance from the village, and near a stream which is called the Meriah stream—a place at all other times carefully avoided by the people. A post is fixed in the centre of the ground. The victim is tied to it, and is then anointed with oil, ghee, and turmeric, and adorned with flowers, and a kind of adoration is paid to him. In some parts rude images of birds and beasts in clay or wood are made, and stuck up on poles.[1]

The sheep led to Mecca by the heathen

[1] Macpherson, p. 114.

ALL KILLING SACRIFICIAL.

Arabs to be sacrificed had garlands or green boughs hung round its neck, that it might be distinguished as a thing sacred.[1]

This is nothing but reminiscence and survival of the adorned human victim among the early Arabs as among the Khonds and others. As we have seen, the Hebrews at first allowed no killing of animals whatever without consecration. The idolatrous Arabs also, in killing any animal for food, were used to consecrate it to their idols by saying, "In the name of Allâ" or "al Uzza." The consecration here implied converted the animal into the *theanthropic* animal of Professor Robertson Smith.

And sometimes the same idea works to very different manifestations. Thus the Tupinambas of Brazil gave certain of their women to male captives, and *ate the children begotten of them*, after sacrifice, as the flesh and blood of enemies — the very opposite of the Meriah sacrifice, yet

---

[1] Koran, sura v. 2nd sentence.

OFFERING AND SACRIFICE.

springing from the self-same motive. The Meriah women, certain of them, were, as hinted, allowed to live till they had borne children to Khond fathers (to have had such children was accounted to them a distinction); and these children were Meriahs, and were put to death in sacrifice, precisely the same as the children begotten of Meriah fathers.

Mr. George Dobson, who lived for a number of years in West Africa, and did not a little to open up commercial relations with tribes on the Volta and the Cameroons, tells me that in Bonny white was the sacred colour, and that when a human sacrifice was made in Opobo (to which King Ja Ja emigrated from Bonny) they procured the very lightest colour they could, as near to white as possible. One, a boy, was sacrificed in 1871 or 1872, when the first vessel anchored in the river; and another, a girl, in 1873, on the bar, to induce other English firms to come and open trade. Within twelve months, Mr. Dobson remarks, four large firms did open

MR. DOBSON'S FACTS.

trade there! But when, in 1883, King Ja Ja, for like objects, repeated the same ceremony, he was taken to task and exiled to the West Indies.

Now, the preference of the lightness or whiteness in these sacrificial victims suggests a question. We have seen that in the case of those sacrificed by the Khonds of Orissa it was imperatively demanded that they should be of another race—that they should be bought with money, as being thus more precious, hard to get. Did this lightness or whiteness preferred in the Bonny victims point to the same idea, though only as a survival? I should be exceedingly glad if any one could enlighten me as to the reason or underlying idea. The likenesses that come out in the most distant peoples, when studying their religious customs, is what astonishes me, for the likenesses are far more wonderful than are the differences. A further reference to Mr. Dobson brought this paragraph:

"The people of the Niger Coast (in

OFFERING AND SACRIFICE.

which now we should be specially interested, since Mr. Chamberlain is one of its saviours and evangelists) do not keep up their population by reproduction. A chief having thirty or forty wives can only boast of three or four children. They buy boys and girls from the interior, and bring them up as their children, and give the girls in marriage to their chiefs and friends, as is done elsewhere with daughters. Hence the sacrifice—the only one I saw—a girl of about fourteen, who was brought for that purpose from the interior. Their self-imposed duty was to get the best they could, and in this case they had done so. The king told me, in the course of my remonstrances with him, that it must be the best thing they could find, otherwise it would be of no avail. He said that when he lived at Bonny one sacrifice was not accepted by the god as not good enough. This sacrifice was for trade. No other human sacrifices were made, except prisoners of war, who were brought to the temple, where they were beheaded, and the body cut up for distribution to be eaten, and the head retained to deck the temple with. The lightness of skin in the sacrifice above mentioned went with the better features, showing traces of mixture with other than pure negro blood."

There can be no doubt that human sacrifices at one time prevailed among the Dyaks of Borneo. To this day the blood of the slain victim is sprinkled over the fields of a farm, with the idea of promoting fertility. And the correspondence here to the Khond business is not far to seek, if the sacrifice be but viewed as a substitution, which indeed it is.[1]

From another point of view, we find Mr. H. Ling Roth demonstrating the same thing. He holds that savages in the lowest scale make no slaves, but eat or sacrifice their captives; that tribes who have made some advance in the arts, even without becoming husbandmen, commence to make slaves of prisoners of war, and

[1] H. Ling Roth, "Natives of Sarawak and Borneo," i. p. 190.

OFFERING AND SACRIFICE.

that agricultural tribes make slavery an institution.[1]

One of the most noticeable festivals of the Chinese is that in which by a procession the clay images of a ploughman and his ox are brought into the city and worshipped. They are carried, on separate wooden platforms, on the shoulders of men specially appointed for the task. They are kept till next day in one of the temples, and are blessed and adored, and then they are broken in pieces in the hall devoted to the god of the passing year. Some of the pieces are religiously kept for *luck*; others are buried in the ground.[2]

Now, this, for very good reasons, could not have been the original observance. It is a survival pointing far, far back, doubtless to the time when the Chinese, like the Khonds, slew an ox and a human victim, and buried parts of the flesh in the earth, to secure, as they thought, the fertility of the land. Keeping clay images of this

---

[1] "Origin of Agriculture," p. 9.
[2] Nevins, p. 143.

AMONG THE CHINESE.

sort for a night in a temple, and worshipping them, is in itself absurd; but it is not absurd as the survival of a rite in which a man and an ox were sacrificed to the Earth-god, or god of rain and moisture, or to conciliate the god of the passing year.

To us it is, indeed, rather surprising to read in the "Athenæum" of June 10th, 1899, reviewing a second edition of Mr. Andrew Lang's "Myth, Ritual, and Religion," the following:

"Historically, we find ancestor-worship more prominent among the Aryans, human sacrifice among the Semites, whilst among the most ancestor-worshipping people the world has ever known, the Chinese, the latter practice is non-existent."

That is fine and far-seeing and exhaustive, especially in view of what we have demonstrated — the clearest survivals of human sacrifice among the Chinese; survivals which else are utterly without any meaning—while among the Aryans, as we find in the Sanskrit, we have the

OFFERING AND SACRIFICE.

clearest evidences in language, and in survivals of *Purushamedha*, human sacrifice. In the words of the Satapatha Brâhmana, *the sacrifice is a man*. It matters not what is substituted: *flour* and ghee or the horse are substitutes, and substitutes only—well attested, in the myth which justifies horse-sacrifice as a substitute, in the human being devoted to sacrifice running away and being transformed into a horse; while among the Semites the proofs of ancestor-worship are absolutely pervasive, and not to be got rid of, in spite of all efforts at veiling the traces made by the Hebrew revisers, English revisers, and all. And what I should say is, that the " Athenæum " writer had but too much bolted Sir Henry Maine, etc., without looking *into* him, and into facts and documents, and so made rather a puzzle of it—so bad that F. Hommel becomes Homme, though that may be a printer's error, which, however, should not have been passed in the leading " Athenæum," which is frequently so very

THE CORN-SPIRIT.

severe on little lapses and slips of the same kind, especially in the cases of those who have as yet no great name to work a charm.

In any great danger or strait the early Greeks were used to vow the sacrifice of a son or a daughter. So, it is clear enough, was the case with the Syrians and other Semitic races, as seen in the Bible itself—notably in the case of the king of Moab, who, in the midst of battle with the Hebrews, offered or passed his son through the fire on the wall, which implied afterwards the sacrificial eating.

The flour of the grain of the last sheaf was supposed by many peoples to contain the corn-spirit, and was eaten ceremonially—a kind of god-eating.

The incarnation of the god in the Roman religion led to customs which distinctly point in the same direction, surrounding the priests, who are feigned to have a mystic identity with the god, with all the elaborate guardianship of *tabus*. The divine being had to be

OFFERING AND SACRIFICE.

guarded because of its embodiment, and lest it should suffer through any accident to the incarnating body or person, which could not be suffered to die a natural death, lest the god should also pay the penalty of mortality. The man-god was sacrificed while yet in full strength, in order that the god might find incarnation in new and yet more powerful forms, while the body was disposed of precisely as in other cases, to aid the growth that was most welcome to the corn-god. The whole process of thought which led to *beans* being regarded with a kind of religious reverence was related also to this idea and to god-eating. "Beans were believed by the Romans to contain the souls of the dead"; and Mr. Jevons remarks that "the object of eating beans at funeral banquets was to convey the powers of the deceased to the kinsmen." Beans were *tabu* to the Flamen Dialis, who must not go near them; he was forbidden to eat of them, or even to name them. Beans were used in making sacrifices to

CICERO'S NOTION.

the dead, *parentando*, because the souls of the dead are in them.[1]

Cicero saw in the Roman sacrifices exactly this phenomenon, which is proved by his asking, in a kind of hidden satiric way, the following: "Who is there who has yet discovered a race of men so destitute of understanding as actually to believe that the things they eat, and give sustenance to their bodies, are their gods?"[2]

The prophet Daniel had understanding in all visions and dreams, and this, inferentially, because he (and his three friends) did not eat of the king's meat or drink of the king's wine,[3] but ate only pulse and drank only water. This is exactly like the medicine men of some North American tribes, as well as Australians, who, before certain ceremonies and advisings about going to war, etc., etc., eat only, or profess to eat only, bread (or pulse) and water; and with the Romans beans, which were

[1] Dr. F. Granger, "The Worship of the Romans."
[2] "De Natura," lib. iii.
[3] Dan. i. 17.

OFFERING AND SACRIFICE.

ordinarily *tabu* to the Flamen Dialis, yet were systematically eaten at funeral banquets.

Much is made of the intimations of immortality in the end of the Book of Daniel; but Daniel, if you hold to individual authorship, had been in contact with Babylonians and Assyrians, and Medes and Persians, and it may even be Egyptians, for they were all to be found where he was.

And Daniel's god, whoever he was, was a trafficker in visions and dreams and their interpretations—a fellow with a diviner's or magician's rod, indeed, in the fullest sense of the words; a pedlar in mysteries and in " wonders generally." Most transparently the whole book is a poor invention—an attempt to magnify the Jewish god, and does it very poorly.

PART II.

CORROBORATIVE TESTIMONY.

II.—CORROBORATIVE TESTIMONY.

VII.

Since this was written, Professor Flinders Petrie's article, "Eaten with Honour," has appeared in the "Contemporary Review" for June, 1897. There is much of value in that article, because the Professor has some real knowledge and observation of his own about Egyptian matters of some 3500 B.C.—the time of the early pyramid builders—to impart to us; but he is a little too easy-going when he surveys mankind from China to Peru and generalises thus : " Higher motives of honour and kindness prevail mostly in Asia, Australia, and South America, but *seem to be unknown* in Polynesia, North America, and Africa." Why, he himself tells us of

OFFERING AND SACRIFICE.

one "little rift within the lute, a little pitted speck in garnered fruit," in the Tlinklets [Thinklets, not Tlinklets] of North America, who "consumed their bravest," with the belief doubtless that their strength and capability would pass into the eaters. Things are far more "mixed" anthropologically than to justify Professor Flinders Petrie or any other from drawing a bold line across the earth like this. Besides, why did he title his article "Eaten with Honour," when, according to him or his German original, exactly one half geographically and on "scientific reckoning" is *not* "eaten with honour," but the reverse? This is his table of classification of motives to cannibalism :

	Per cent.	
Honour, kindness, future good, love	20	
To obtain strength or magic results .	19	
As a ceremony to acquire position .	10	
As a punishment (? to eater or the eaten)	5	
		54
From hunger or need of food . .	18	
From preference as food . . .	28	
		46
		100

"TOUGH OLD FELLOWS."

Now, Professor Flinders Petrie is guilty of the enormity of declaring, in his generalised statement, that "eaten with honour" *seems* to be unknown in Africa, whilst he declares the direct opposite of the very Libyans who, he says, communicated the habit to the Egyptians. As to Australia, the Professor quotes from another thus: "But the men are still eaten, especially chiefs; and I have heard of cases recently where tough, skinny old fellows have been faithfully eaten, although they could not have been very juicy. The reason, I am told, is that by partaking of the flesh of a person they inherit the virtues of that person." And then he proceeds to say that, from all the circumstances, the Egyptian cases were clearly in motive, etc., similar to this. He writes: "The arranging of the bones into the semblance of the body shows extreme care, which must prevent our looking on this as otherwise than a reverent and honoured burial"; and the motives to the cannibalism could not have been different,

OFFERING AND SACRIFICE.

he says, from those of the Australians. Well, but then what of the pronouncement absolutely on Africa?

And then did Professor Flinders Petrie really think out what is implied in this sentence with strict reference to his classification above: " More than half the dead who are eaten, and *in most cases* when people are killed it is the aged, sickly, and infirm—the *killing of the young and healthy is an aberration unknown in most lands*"? I much fear he did not. He puts down as " From preference as food, 28," and " from hunger or need of food, 18 "—a very large percentage, almost one-half of the whole, and yet, according to his fine generalisation here, they act, every man-jack of them, altogether unnaturally; they leave, he says, the tender tit-bits—the infants, the young and robust—and tackle the old and tough—the old and tough, and the sickly and the dying, practically over the whole area. Is that according to human nature and human preference? That is what I want to know. Failing Professor Flinders

THE ATTICOTTIS.

Petrie, will Mr. Percy W. Bunting tell me what I want to know? If Professor Flinders Petrie will exhaustively and satisfactorily answer this, I shall admit him a fine comparative anthropologist and *thinker* as well as a careful Egyptologist and skilful excavator and explorer; and if, failing Professor Flinders Petrie, Mr. Percy W. Bunting will do it, then I shall declare him a fine thinker and noble writer as well as an expert editor and great lawyer.

Professor Flinders Petrie, in addition to his other lapses, quotes a description from St. Jerome of the Atticotti, a British tribe, as preferring human flesh to that of cattle. But there is always a good deal to be qualified in the reports of saints or missionaries, old or new, about heathens and heathen habits, even if there is no mistake in the matter. But it turns out that there is good reason—good reason—for believing that St. Jerome was in this case seriously misled by a wrong translation: and if Professor Flinders Petrie wants an authority, he will find it in Villaneuva, i. p. 245.

OFFERING AND SACRIFICE.

There is indeed a relief in getting any ground for saying and thinking that the Atticotti were not so bad as they have been painted—as Professor Flinders Petrie even at this time of day has once more painted them; but he must look to Villa-neuva, where, we fancy, he will find set down together the original and the translation.[1]

See also, to much the same effect, Borlase, " Dolmens of Ireland," ii. pp. 474-6. He holds that, precisely like other races, the Atticotti were once eaters of human sacrifices, but that in Jerome's time they were certainly not so, and that Jerome's words are false and libellous, and surely no better, as ignorantly quoted by Professor Flinders Petrie.

We much prefer Mr. Borlase's explanation to that of Professor Flinders Petrie; it is more philosophical—goes far deeper.

At the root of it all lay the cultus of the dead, and there is no need to shun the fact that in the British Islands, in the

Atticotti = *giant* men, though sometimes it has been given as ancient men.

days when the inhabitants were little different from other savage peoples of Northern Europe, human sacrifices, almost certainly combined with cannibal practices, prevailed. There is also something important about the Atticotti in Professor Rhys's " Celtic Britain."

VIII.

In fact, the idea that really underlies the Khond sacrifice is common—only differing from other phases in some points of development. Major Macpherson notes that the great object in some of the cruel points in the process was to draw as many tears as possible from the victim, in the belief that the cruel Tári would proportionately increase the supply of rain! Hence the significance of this sentence: " The Khonds believed that the flesh of the victim fertilised the land, the blood produced the redness of the turmeric, and the tears brought rain."

The Oorigas of Burma, who migrated to

OFFERING AND SACRIFICE.

Burma from Gopalpur, have a custom of human sacrifices exactly like that of the Khonds. They also are to propitiate Tarri Pennu, the Earth-goddess, that she may favour agriculture. The victim's blood and pieces of the flesh are distributed amongst the bystanders, and spread over the fields. Human sacrifices are also made if there is an epidemic of fever or smallpox, or if there is a plague. But they have many and high virtues.[1]

In Mangaia the same significance was attached to the destination of certain portions of the human sacrifice. "All the district chiefs and landowners received from the king a portion of the ears of the victim wrapped up in a *ti* leaf. . . . These bits of human ears were deposited in the different family maraes. They constituted an investiture to all offices and *right to the possession of the soil.*" Very possibly, as with the Khonds of Orissa, some of them were planted in land; but, however that may be, they were certainly

[1] "Burma Census Report," Introduction, p. 339.

THE PAWNEES.

identified with it, and wherever placed were presumed to favour fruitfulness, and to favour peace which was essential to fruitfulness. "The man who had the management of all great feasts, and *was supposed to make the food grow, came in for his share of the nose.*" And thus the great lay:

> "A bleeding victim has been chosen for our altar;
> By it are weeded out the evils of the land."

So that here, just as in the case of the Khonds, we have a kind of indirect god-eating.[1] So also have we in the sacred eating of bread among the Aztecs.

We read at Exod. xxiii. 19: "Thou shalt not seethe a kid in his mother's milk"; which is not due, as often represented, to any sense of justice and dislike of cruelty to animals, but to the fact that such milk was used for superstitious lustrations of the fields—the modification of an older practice which points to the same thing as the Khond sacrifice buried in earth.

The Pawnees annually sacrificed a

[1] Wyatt Gill, "Myths and Songs," p. 297.

OFFERING AND SACRIFICE.

human victim in the spring, when they sowed or planted their fields. We are told of one such observance—the sacrifice of a girl: "While her flesh was still warm, it was cut in small pieces from the bones, put in little baskets, and taken to a neighbouring cornfield. Here the head chief took a piece of the flesh from a basket, and squeezed a drop of blood upon the newly-deposited grains of corn. His example was followed by the rest, till all the seed had been sprinkled with blood; it was then covered up with earth."

Mr. Chalmers tells that when the natives of New Guinea begin planting, they first take a bunch of bananas and sugar-cane, and go to the centre of the plantation and call over the names of the dead belonging to the family, adding, "There is your food, your bananas and sugar-cane; let our food grow well, and let it be plentiful." There is the greatest reason for thinking that originally banana and sugar-cane were the totems of these tribes, so that here, too, is a god-eating as with the Roman beans.

MULTIPLICATION OF RELICS.

The relics of chiefs and kings in earlier times in many places were actually cut up and divided out, so that the sanctity thus expressed might have centres far apart from each other. This was the origin of the *stupa* among the Hindus, of the Greek mound, of the Chinese gravemound, of the mounds of America. In the heart of each was the body, or part of the body, or relic of a saint, hero, or ancestor. Buddha's body and relics were cut up and divided among chiefs and kings, and *stupas* were built over them in various places. The body of Osiris was cut up into a number of pieces by Typhon, and Isis found them and built a temple over each. Here we have legends founded on what was, no doubt, a practice of early peoples, who cut up the human sacrifice and so honoured it; the Khond sacrifice and its division into parts being merely another form of the same tendency—the earth being consecrated and blessed by its reception. Here we have, in part at all events, the secret of the multiplication of holy relics.

OFFERING AND SACRIFICE.

Dr. Edkins, the well-known Chinese missionary and scholar, writes to the effect that the Confucian and Taouist temples are but an edition of the houses, only they contain a relic, a statue or tablet to the god: " The prevailing character of these and other temples belonging to the Confucian religion is funereal. They are the abodes of the dead. The name of the tablet—Shin-wei or Ling-wei, 'the place of the soul'—denotes that the spirit is supposed to be present there. . . . The Taouist temples, like the Confucian, are intended for honour to the dead."

Among the Mayas, who inhabited Mexico, Guatemala, and Yucatan prior to the Aztecs and Toltecs, the cross was a symbol, which the conquerors adopted from the conquered. It was the emblem of Quiateot, the god of rain. In order to obtain rain little boys and girls were sacrificed to him, and their flesh devoured at a sacred banquet by the chiefs.[1]

[1] The numerous cases in which images of clay are now used by different tribes to induce rain are clearly

THE SUN-SIGN.

Now here, as in some other cases, the cross symbol is associated with water, with rain, with moisture, with fertility. It was so also in the arkite symbol; here it is in connection with sacrifices to the rain-god; and as the hammer of Thor or the lightning, it is not far-off. What does Mr. Baring-Gould say to this? Why, on the most important of the drawings he gives in his plate of illustrations, down the centre of his cross is a fish disguised under a tree-branch—a phallic symbol—and we know what such symbol means. We may touch on this in a later volume, when treating of the genesis and evolution of the Tau, but to do it here would lead to great disproportion.

The truth is, the sign of the cross was, as we have seen, the sun-sign, and, secondly, the crossing which was and is

survivals from a time when human victims were sacrificed for the same purpose. Intercourse by sea between ancient America and the Mediterranean is held by some to be proved by the hitherto unnoticed lotus patterns of ancient Mexico and Yucatan and of the modern Zuni Indians, whose culture is known to be a survival from early prehistoric times. But likeness in symbols of this kind are not what should in themselves be taken as proof of such intercourse.

OFFERING AND SACRIFICE.

determined by the full moon of Easter—the contact of the male and female—the cross was re-erected with the entry of the vernal equinox—the crossing into light, heat, and warmth—life and growth and beauty. As the sun-sign it constantly involves itself with the phallic sign, †; see Payne Knight's "Worship of Priapus." On certain vases, &c., Pan is represented as pouring water on the o. o. g., invigorating the active creative power by the prolific element in which it acted.

Rizpah watches the bodies of her sons that had been hung up before Jahvé—*hung up before Jahvé*—till rain comes in assurance that Israel had, by human sacrifice, atoned for the crime of Saul. It was only the conduct of Rizpah which so touched David that he gathered together the bones and had them buried at Zelah, in the sepulchre of Kish, the father of Saul. Joshua (viii. 29) hangs the king of Ai on a tree until evening, and as soon as the sun was down Joshua commanded that they should take his carcase down from the tree—not to

DATE OF DEUTERONOMY.

bury it, but to cast it at the entering of the gate of the city and raise a heap of stones on it. So with the five combined kings. Joshua hung them on trees, and took them down at the going down of the sun and cast them into the cave where they had been hid, and laid a great stone on the cave mouth. It is clear that the Deuteronomic law was not then in force, *if the Deuteronomic code so much as existed* (of course, Wellhausen, Kuenen, and the rest are firm in the opinion that it was not in existence till very much later), for all this is in direct opposition to it, unless we are to insert a negative in this passage (Deut. xxi. 22, 23): "And if a man have committed a sin worthy of death, and he be to be put to death, and thou hang him on a tree, his body shall not remain all night upon the tree : but thou shalt [not] in any wise bury him that day (for he that is hanged is accursed of God), that thy land be not defiled, which the Lord thy God giveth thee for an inheritance."[1]

[1] Colenso rightly points out that here we have a proof that, if the Deuteronomic legislation was known

OFFERING AND SACRIFICE.

The dead were by the early Hebrews thought to exist in Sheol in precisely the same condition as in the moment of dying; hence, like Abimelech and Saul, men would kill themselves rather than pass into the hands of enemies. As a result of this process of thought, those who were hanged could not enter Sheol, because their bodies could not be buried — to leave a body unburied or to throw it to dogs was the greatest insult that could be done to an

to David, he acted directly in opposition to it. The slaying or "offering" of Saul's sons was directly a violation of this law: "The fathers shall not be put to death for the children, neither shall the children be put to death for the fathers: every man shall be put to death for his own sin" (Deut. xxiv. 16); and the exposure of the corpses for many days (2 Sam. xxi. 10) was as directly a violation of the laws laid down in both codes. So that it is hard to see how it could be said that David obeyed the law of his god, if these codes were known to him—facts which seem to give full support to the assertion that before the time of Samuel Israel had no political or religious organisation whatever; and further that, as Oort demonstrates (p. 9), "There was no lawful official worship in Israel before the time of David, if even in the full sense it could be said to have existed before the time of Josiah and the *alleged* discovery of that Book of the Covenant, when the Passover was celebrated as it had never been before in Israel—the last clause being really "never before celebrated in Israel."

SACRIFICE AND RAIN.

enemy. The spirits of the unburied were thought to roam restlessly about the spot where the body was, and to put an end to this, it may be, the heaping up of stones over the unburied body of an enemy was had recourse to; hence the origin of the גַּלִּים, heaps of stones, according to Gesenius.

Joshua and David, anyhow, did not bury on the same night the bodies of those whom they had caused to be hanged. Now, if so much weight was laid on the idea that the land was not to be defiled by burying in it those who were hanged as malefactors, are we not justified in inferring an idea of blessing to the earth in burying in it those who had been accepted, and also, it may be, parts of those who had been devoted and offered in sacrifice? At all events, all those sacrifices were held, as were the Meriah sacrifices and those of the Mayas, in close connection with the idea of procuring rain and blessing and fruitfulness to the land, that indirect god-eating might be realised.

OFFERING AND SACRIFICE.

With the Pawnee Indians, as Mr. Grinnell tells, though *Atius Tiráwa* is the supreme god, the omnipotent and beneficent, pervading the universe (*Atius* being father and *Tiráwa* spirit), the Pawnees have many other subsidiary gods. The earth is sacred, and is worshipped as " the father of the dead." It is through the dead buried in its bosom that the earth is rich and fruitful; for alongside of Father Earth is the female deity " Mother Corn." " Just as the white people talk about Jesus Christ," said a Bee priest to Mr. Grinnell, " so we talk about the corn."[1] It is their saviour, in a sense, their mediator—it is the first representative to them of the supreme god, *Atius Tiráwa*; and when they eat of the fruits of the earth, they are eating

[1] " The Story of the Indians," by George Bird Grinnell. Mr. Grinnell says of the Pawnee religion : " On the whole, so far as I understand it, it is a singularly pure faith, and in its essential features will compare favourably with any savage system. If written in our sacred books, the trust and submission to the will of the Ruler shown in some of the myths, which I have elsewhere recorded, would be called sublime."

MR. ANDREW LANG.

of what the dead have contributed to yield in their union with Father Earth—father of the dead—and so their ordinary meals, too, are, in a sense, god-eating.

Mr. Andrew Lang has dealt with "god-eating"—in the most passing manner, however—in a paragraph or two in his chapter "Mexican Divine Myths," in "Myth, Ritual, and Religion," pp. 73-75. There he concerns himself almost entirely with the Mexican phenomena, or, at all events, all that he says takes rise from them, though why the matter should thus have been ranked as primarily Mexican goes beyond me. But Mr. Lang does rise to a general statement or two. "The custom of god-eating is common amongst totemistic peoples, who, except on this solemn occasion, abstain from [eating] their totem. Müller mentions (*Ur-Am. Rel.*) a dog tribe in Arkansas which sacramentally eat dogs' flesh. *This rite may be regarded as a commutation of cannibalism*" (italics are mine). But certainly he declines to see much of god-eating where

OFFERING AND SACRIFICE.

its traces are most patent, when he is so decided in his opinion (and with the full approval of the versatile and most learned Editor of the "Contemporary Review") that the Jewish "passings through the fire" were "harmless rites," and had no connection whatever with god-eating or god-drinking, however remotely.[1]

Mr. Frazer in his "Golden Bough" has tackled the subject in a much more thorough-going manner; but this chapter was written before I had read his book, and I prefer thus to refer to it instead of making any attempt to strengthen my own paper by quotations from it.

God-eating is very definitely connected, as it could not but be, with the idea of unity through covenant. All eating together with heathen men is a bond of brotherhood—the eating of the sacrifice is a special, a sacramental bond—they all become one through identity with the god.

"The home of the clan is the home of its god. The stone god is also at first

[1] "Contemporary Review," August, 1896.

DERIVATION OF "MEXICO."

the altar. There the totem beast is slain; some of its blood is dashed upon the stone, and around it the rest of the blood is drunk and the flesh is eaten by the clansmen. This is probably the primitive form of sacrifice. It is not a gift to the god, but a sacrament in which the whole kin— the god with his clansmen—unites. In partaking of it each member of the kin testifies and renews his union with the rest. The god himself is eaten, and yet he is at the same time embodied in the sacred stone." Blood was the share of the totem god in all sacrificial feasts.[1]

The most extraordinary instance of definite yet symbolic god-eating is thus set forth by Dr. E. B. Tylor in his "Primitive Culture":

"The very name of Mexico seems to be derived from Mexitli, the national war-god, identical or identified with the hideous gory Huitzilopochtli. Not to attempt a general solution of the enigmatic nature of this inextricable compound

[1] Hartland, "Perseus," ii. p. 236.

OFFERING AND SACRIFICE.

parthenogenetic deity, we may notice the association of his principal festival with the winter solstice, when his paste idol was shot through with an arrow, and being thus killed, was divided into morsels and eaten, wherefore the ceremony was called the *teoqualo*, or 'god-eating.' This and other details tend to show Huitzilopochtli as originally a nature-deity, whose life and death were connected with the years, while his functions of war-god may be of later addition."

In fact, he seems to have passed through something of the same process as the Roman Mars.

One survival of the totemistic idea may be traced through the higher phases of sacrifice. The sacred animal — sacred because of its association with the god — is in a certain sense divine, and when after sacrifice it is eaten, something of the very god presumed to be present in it brings it very close to the notion of god-eating.

Sir John Lubbock tells about the

"BAW-DEE-THAT-DO."

great yearly sacrifice in honour of Tezcatlipoca, which was also very remarkable. "Some beautiful youth, usually a war-captive, was chosen as the victim. For a whole year he was treated and worshipped as a god. When he went out he was attended by a numerous train of pages, and the crowd as he passed prostrated themselves before him and did him homage as the impersonation of the great deity. Everything he could wish was provided for him, and at the commencement of the last month four beautiful girls were allotted to him as wives. Finally, when the fatal day arrived, he was placed at the head of a solemn procession, taken to the temple, and after being sacrificed with much ceremony and every token of respect, his heart was offered to the sun and his legs and arms, &c., cooked and eaten by the priests and chiefs."[1]

Mr. J. G. Scott is very careful to tell us about the Burma Baw-dee-that-do, connected with the peculiar process of tattooing

[1] "Origin of Civilisation," p. 240.

OFFERING AND SACRIFICE.

against snake-bite: when undergoing the process they must eat chunks of human flesh. He has much to say about the peculiar result on the Baw-dee-that-do, producing in some cases exceptional powers and tendencies which may be the results of inoculation or may not be; but this peculiar custom most distinctly suggests a survival of sacramental or ceremonial eating of human flesh—undoubtedly another form of godeating, and as decisively telling of a religious basis for the tattooing against snake-bite. Was it originally an initiation into a serpent or poisonous snakeclan or tribe? We ask this with the more justification because we have found traces of an African tribe where the priest's shoulder covering is serpent skins.

That very peculiar process by which Moses made the children of Israel actually eat their golden calf may be significant in this relation too. He took the idol, burned it and ground it to powder, cast it on the water, and made the people drink it! One of the strangest instances of god-

"THE HEAVENLY FAMILY."

eating we have yet come across. But is it likely Moses would have thought of this very peculiar process if something in previous custom or ritual had not suggested it to him?

A very comprehensive designation for divinities of all kinds is "ta anau tua-rangi," or *the-heavenly-family* ("tu-a-rangi" = like-the-heaven-or-sky). Strangely enough, this celestial race includes rats, lizards, beetles, eels, and sharks, and several kinds of birds. The supposition was that "the-heavenly-family" had taken up their abode in these birds, fish, and reptiles—that, in a word, they were once totems. (Gill, "Myths and Songs," p. 52.)

The people of Encounter Bay in Australia suppose that nearly all the animals have been anciently men who performed great prodigies, and at last transformed themselves into animals and stones. (J. D. Woods, p. 202.)

Here is one exceptional case, the same belief presenting the very opposite results in practice:

"The Tuscaroras did not eat rabbit or

OFFERING AND SACRIFICE.

ground-hog; they fancied they were related to them." (Heckwelder, p. 252.)

Or was it that they ate them only as holy food like the rest?

IX.

It is very remarkable how often that idea of strength, as associated with the dead, occurs even in the Hebrew. For instance, we have רָפָא, רְפָאִים, departed shades, dead men. From the root directly comes weak or feeble—only, however, on the principle Professor Bain has laid down; for it significantly gives also רָפָא, strong, to be strong, tall, of giant size: hence רְפָאִים, giants. From the same root comes, too (in fact, it is but another form of the selfsame word), רָפָא, to cure, to heal; and the very word רֹפֵא, a physician, is from the same source. רָפָה is but another form of the verb to heal, or make strong; and in antithesis to this we have again, on Professor Bain's principle,

DR. PEROWNE'S COMMENT.

רָפָה, to sink or fall down, to become faint, unnerved, or to look deathlike. רָפָא (in 2 Sam. xxi. 16 and 18) is the Hebrew for "the giant" in the Authorised Version. רְפָאֵל might thus, perhaps, admit of another interpretation than *El heals*. In short, to our idea, the whole development of the group of words from this root would lead us to the idea that the Hebrews, like many other peoples, had shared in some of the stages of life in which strength was presumed to lie in feasting on the dead, and so gaining strength, becoming powerful and big.

And when we refer back to Lev. xxvii. 28 and 29, where even in the legislation as it stands human sacrifice is clearly commanded, are we to assume that in any form these sacrifices were eaten?

In his comment on Psalm lxxxviii. 10, "Shall the shades below" (that is, ancestors) "arise and give thee thanks?" Dr. Perowne has this particularly unsatisfactory and half-and-half comment: רְפָאִים: here the spirits of the departed, εἴδωλα

OFFERING AND SACRIFICE.

καμόντων, comp. Isa. xxvi. 14, Prov. xxi. 16, &c., but in other places used of "the race of giants." Many attempts have been made to connect the two significations (see Gesen. Thes. in v.), but perhaps Hupfeld's is the most plausible. He connects the word with the root רפה, *to be relaxed*, and so (*a*) weak, feeble as "the shades," and on the other (*b*) *extended*, at a vast length, *immania corpora*, like "the giants." Jerome here has *gigantes*; "the LXX. ἰατροί, connecting it curiously with the root רפא, to heal. רפהים is also used in the same sense at Job xxvi. 5 and Isa. xiv. 9.[1]

Much here might have been made of the use of the word נפש without מת for the dead, the departed—a thing which we have attended to in detail elsewhere. The phrase להם נפש has then a very special and a very peculiar significance, and I would fain press home on preachers and teachers like Principal Fairbairn practically to

---

[1] The Hebrew word from which giant has been translated signifies "to fall."

SUGGESTIVE WORDS.

elucidate and explain this to me in consistency with their more exoteric teachings.

Very significant it is, too, to trace חיל and גְּבִיר in the same way. Take the first. חיל is used for power, as at 1 Chron. xxvi. 7; while in verse 6 the word גִּבּוֹרֵי is used for the same thing. We have בְּנֵי־חַיִל, sons of power or might, which is translated " men of might."

In the same way the Hebrews have no word to describe " valour " in the case of Jephthah save this same word, חַיִל. We read (Judges xi. 1) הָיָה גִּבּוֹר חַיִל—a mighty man of valour. Now it is very peculiar that, as in many other cases, an earlier meaning still lingers in a poetical use, and this is vigour of tree-life—strength of leaf and fruit, productiveness. Here we have lingering in the poetical sense and usage a reminiscence of the tree-*numen*, as we have it in so many other cases, אֵל, etc., etc.

Further, it is remarkable that this word חַיִל, with its original suggestion of tree-

OFFERING AND SACRIFICE.

strength, productiveness, is used for a good, virtuous, or worthy woman. In Ruth iii. 11, as well as in the 10th verse of Proverbs xxxi., the beautiful anagrammatic passage in praise of a good wife, we have אֵשֶׁת חַיִל.

The word טוֹב, which is given as meaning *good*, in the widest sense, traces to a root which clearly shows that this word originally had reference to land—and that naturally it has reference primarily only to external good, or to delights of sense, and only by a strain can it be applied to what is inward and of the spirit—subjective quality, in a word, although in a few cases it is so applied. This all surely goes to show decided poverty in the expression of inward qualities of character in a *lingua sacra*.

In the very idea of the Hoama and Soma is implied the conception of a god present—the god becomes the drink, or the drink is conceived to have become the god. The sacred drink confers immortality: this is a refined form of the

THE REAL PRESENCE.

idea of the god being partaken of; some of his power passes into the eater or the drinker. Even in the idea of eating or drinking *with* the god there was a suggestion of strength or of grace, which is but another form of strength conferred. Even in the Hebrew, favour was found in God's sight through the rich and readily-offered sacrifices—the sweet savour of the sacrifice was well-pleasing to God, and in that very fact lay the imagined lifting-up and beatifying of those who had rendered the sacrifices. The sacred meal in which the god was present has, in one form or another, been so common that it may almost be regarded as ethnic; and certainly, then, when we hear of transubstantiation and the Real Presence in the sacraments of the Christian Church, we see only an elaborated and thinly-spiritualised form of the god-eating and god-drinking of very early and sometimes very rude and savage people. Truly, in this sense also, there is nothing new under the sun.

OFFERING AND SACRIFICE.

X.

Scarce anything of late years has caused me more amused reflection, as may be inferred from what I have said already, than the petition of certain Anglicans to the Pope for recognition of Anglican Orders. What is it really that these good men applied for? Nothing less than to be transported back into blackest heathenism, and anew entitled to set up their priests as the agents for the encouragement of what, in some phases, was the most debased of heathen practices—god-eating and god-drinking. The power of the Roman Catholic priest, in relation to the sacrament of the Lord's Supper, is nothing more nor less than this: A chief priest, so-called Pope, resident in Rome, claims alone to have the power (as nearly all the priests or popes of heathen antiquity claimed) of so consecrating the sacrifice that the partaking of it was really god-eating. What else, in reality, does the Pope claim? Nothing else: he claims

OLD PRIESTLY CLAIM.

that. The main reason given in the recent Papal Bull on the authenticity of English Orders itself was that Anglican Orders were invalid in the Roman sense of the word; that is to say, that they did not possess the nature and effect of a sacrament, and, in particular, that they carried with them *no power of consecrating and offering the true body and blood of the Lord as a sacrifice to the* ETERNAL FATHER.

What more do you want? If that is not the revival by mumbo-jumbo of the old heathen priestly claim I do not know what it is. The triple-hatted Papa in St. Peter's knows that as well as anybody, or, if he doesn't, then he wants to renew his youth and study Hebrew and Sanskrit and many allied tongues and religions; as certainly do some of our own English busybodies, among them the Archbishops of Canterbury and York— Temple, one of the writers of " Essays and Reviews," and there a disher-up of half-and-half Lessingism; and Maclagan of York, some say an " old soldier—who wanted

OFFERING AND SACRIFICE.

this Pope to say that Anglican priests had the same power as he claims of heathen humbug and mumbo-jumbo. It would become them far, far better to do something to get the needed discipline in their Church, and to make it ordinarily decent. Many of their priests are already too much in league with Jezebels, painted Jezebels, and nobody can do anything to make them shake them off, either.

And this matter goes even a point further. When you come to give a class of men a power such as this, you find that it soon allies itself with a claim to enforce the acceptance of it even by pains or by penalties. Salvation depends upon this acceptance—absolutely depends upon it; and the next step, power being obtained, is to kill off or to exterminate those who will not accept it. Such was the result—and quite the logical result—of Roman Catholicism at certain eras of history, which, mainly on account of this claim, took occasion by the hand "with rack and screw, the boot and fire." The

DR. FREEMAN'S WORD.

serious inconsistency of men who politically go for individual freedom, enfranchisement, equality, and independence of judgment, and yet would fain have the Pope to acknowledge this power as resident in their Anglican religious teachers, does not need much pointing out. Some of them go hard on Turks, and yet would arm Romish and Romanising priests with the very " consecration " which has invariably, in one form or another, accompanied and egged on to persecution and massacre. This is no theory; it is history broadwrit over Europe at certain times, as Dr. Freeman, by-the-bye, for one, never failed to say.

Mr. C. Kegan Paul, once a scholar of Charles Kingsley, then a Broad Church priest in the English Church, and after that a publisher, and now one of the devoutest of the devout among English Roman Catholics (and surely the publisher's enterprise was a delightfully spacious " Bridge of Sighs" connecting the two distant regions of cloud and mystery), writing

OFFERING AND SACRIFICE

in the "Cornhill Magazine" for November, 1896, says that Huysman's words are true when he asserts that " Free-thought, Black Masses, *Satanism*, and Freemasonry are closely connected." But some deduction may need to be made even on such a judgment from one who, in England, at the end of the nineteenth century, declares that "with all my heart I desire to obey the deliberate voice of the Popes, who speak with authority given to no other than the Vicars of Christ alone." Poor, poor, poor Mr. Kegan Paul! What a splendid subject for his pen for the next few years, the kissing of the Pope's toe, and its origin. That, indeed, is something which Mr. Kegan Paul and his co-Romanists should carefully study.

At this moment, as we have seen in the Church of England, a whole party, by the re-institution of a priestly sacrifice, carries us back to the heathen form of god-eating and god-drinking: first the sacrifice is offered to the god, who, by becoming one with the sacrifice at the

ST. MATTHEW'S, WESTMINSTER.

prayer of the priest, consecrates it; then it is eaten and drunken—the body and blood of the god. A correspondent of the "Daily Chronicle," who has done a tour of such churches, and described their services, has this in effect to say of them all; and here is the special description of a part of the service at St. Matthew's, Westminster:

"The instructions and prayers in the Eucharistic part were perfectly frank. Before the Prayer for the Church Militant the child was told that at this point 'the priest puts bread and wine on the altar, and offers them to God,' and then followed a prayer, 'Accept, O Holy Father, the sacrifice which Thy priest is about to offer to Thee.' Before the Consecration the children said, 'Send down Thy Holy Spirit upon this Sacrifice that He may make this bread the Body of Thy Christ, and this cup the Blood of Thy Christ.' And after the Consecration, 'We offer unto Thee the Body and Blood of Thy Son Jesus Christ here present on Thy holy

OFFERING AND SACRIFICE.

altar, the one perfect Sacrifice for the sins of the whole world.'"

If this is possible in the Church of England, all we can say is that she is in no sense reformed—that she has all the disadvantages without any of the advantages of Rome, in which the discipline is at least what it pretends to be; and if, as we understand, one bishop has said that a national Church should have something for every *taste*—*taste*, mark you—then, assuredly, it amply provides for a disguised pagan or savage taste, though its priests may not only marry, but, as Sir Walter Scott said, "may dae waur," and no one deal with them—that is something for every one's *taste*. And Mr. Balfour, the abounding Mr. Balfour, rejoices!

Lord Hugh Cecil, with a prayer-book in one hand and handy quotations from Sir William Harcourt's volume in the other, and, what is more, with the unctuous and earnest sense of consecration that sits so exceeding well on any one bearing the name of Cecil, told the House of Commons

SPLENDID KEEPERS.

on May 10th, 1899, when speaking on the Church Discipline Bill introduced by Mr. McArthur, that "theirs was a position of trust. *They kept the gates of God's vineyard.*" Who were the they? The general ruck of the elected to Parliament—infidels, disbelievers, &c., among them—the laymen of the Commons, or Hugh Cecil and his friends? Well, no doubt, splendid keepers they are—they know how in everything to *keep things*—as they are. Two questions for Hugh Cecil. First, is he right or are we right historically and absolutely about these masses, transubstantiations, lighted candles, incense, posturings, etc., etc.? Are they, in a direct sense, the survivals of brutal savagery and heathenism in all their forms and phases, or are they not? Are they the glossed-over uprisings of the god-eatings and god-drinkings of utter savagery—in Africa, in Mexico, in Brazil, and in Phœnicia and Palestine—or are they not? Secondly, are bishops more concerned for their big incomes and their big palaces, "meek followers of Jesus," who had not

OFFERING AND SACRIFICE.

where to lay His head, than for order and rule in their Church? They are "*keepers of the gate of God's vineyard*"; but while they keep the gate, if little foxes do not spoil the vines, the vines want pruning or they will not yield. Let them no longer stand at the gate, but go in and prune as long ago they should have done. Hugh Cecil is for freedom, independence, *and* establishment. Is he also for the heathen and savage rites of god-eating and god-drinking, fully revived in England by a set of men who wish to reap the benefits of Parliamentary protection while defying all Parliamentary authority? Honest man! It is not a question of freedom or spiritual independence *alone:* it is to me, at all events, a question of turning back the current of history, and showing the keepers of the gate of God's vineyard as patrons of truly antique customs—god-eating and god-drinking—and the God's vineyard turned at last into something not so unlike an Australian Corrobborree, with holy men doing as little there as they did in old and

DR. EGGELING'S WORDS.

early time, and all paying tribute to their ascendency.

To show how absolutely at one humanity is in this, as, alas! in so much else, I must beg to be allowed to quote the following from Dr. Eggeling's Introduction to the "Satapatha Brâhmana." In the light of it, the step is not far from the Hindu priests to the Anglican priests who are fain to think that Lord Halifax and his friends did them a great service in begging the Pope to say they could consecrate the sacrifice and so promote heathen god-eating and god-drinking:

"The Brâhmanas represent the intellectual activity of a sacerdotal caste which, by turning to account the religious instincts of a gifted and naturally devout race, had succeeded in transforming a primitive worship of the powers of Nature into a highly artificial system of sacrificial ceremonies, and was ever intent on deepening and extending its hold on the minds of the people, by surrounding its own vocation with the halo of sanctity and divine

OFFERING AND SACRIFICE.

inspiration. A complicated ceremonial, requiring for its proper observance and consequent efficacy the ministration of a highly-trained priestly class, has ever been one of the most effective means of promoting hierarchical aspirations." Even practical Rome did not entirely succeed in steering clear of the rock of priestly ascendency attained by suchlike means. There, as elsewhere, the neglect or faulty observance of the worship of each god revenged itself in the corresponding occurrence; and as it was a laborious and difficult task to gain even a knowledge of one's religious obligations, the priests who were skilled in the law of divine things, and pointed out its requirements—the *pontifices*—could not fail to attain an extraordinary influence. (Mommsen, i. p. 181.)[1]

The devout belief in the efficacy of

[1] And it was with unspeakable regret that I read this:—
"NEW BOOK PROMISED SOON.
"A Stockport correspondent having written to Mr. Gladstone on the subject of the Papal Bull as to th

THE RIG-VEDA.

invocation and sacrificial offering which pervades most of the hymns of the Rig-Veda, and which may be assumed to reflect pretty faithfully the religious sentiments of those among whom they were composed, could not but ensure to the priest, endowed with the gift of sacred utterance, a considerable amount of respect and reverence on the part of the people. His superior culture and habitual communion with the divine rulers of the destinies of man would naturally entitle him to a place of honour by the side of the

validity of Anglican Orders, has received the following reply:

"'Dear Sir,—In a few weeks I hope to publish a small volume of facts which will contain what I have to say upon the Papal Bull condemning Anglican Orders. I leave to properly-qualified persons the examination and exposure of his feeble arguments, but I offer a few comments upon the strange want of forethought, courage, and prudence which, while doubtless acting with good intention, he has exhibited.
"Yours very faithfully,
"(Signed)   W. E. GLADSTONE."

I am not aware that this production ever saw the light; and perhaps 'tis well 'tis so. But surely Mr. John Morley will find it hard to reconcile that with much else—not to say, to justify it from his point of view.

OFFERING AND SACRIFICE.

chiefs of clans or the rulers of kingdoms, who would not fail to avail themselves of his spiritual services in order to secure the favour of the gods for their warlike expeditions or political undertakings.[1] And priests are always and everywhere the promoters, if not the creators, of caste. In the Rig-Veda there is, with the single exception of the Purushasûkta, no clear indication of the existence of caste in the proper Brahminical sense of the word."

Priesthoods have ever been promoters of caste: this is enshrined in the Church of England Catechism. To endow them with the same power as Roman Catholic priests while yet they are not celibate, but allied all round with wealthy or aristocratic families, is to open the way to new and worse forms of caste. How do the friends of Mr. Gladstone, the Liberal, the Emancipator, the Reformer, reconcile these two things? I shall be glad to hear.[2]

[1] Eggeling, vol i., pp. x., xi.
[2] This was written while Mr. Gladstone was still alive and active—speaking on behalf of Armenia. It is allowed to stand because there was really nothing

MY HUMBLE OPINION.

And here a word or two about a fact in connection with English Orders, and what is required to secure them. I do not say that a knowledge of Hebrew is essential to the proper performance of much of parson duty as demanded by the Church of England; but I do say that some knowledge of Hebrew is essential to a professed interpreter of so-called " Holy " Scripture. Now I have met with more than one incumbent of the Church of England who did not even know the Hebrew letters. Yet they posed and piqued themselves on their positions as legally authorised interpreters of the Old Testament. My humble opinion is that, if Lord Halifax and his friends had raised an agitation for getting the mass of parsons of the Church of England educated up to *nearly* the level required in Presbyterian and Dissenting Churches, and freed from their firm hold in their freeholds, as Dr. Jessopp would

personal in this question. Mr. Gladstone's friends are bound to find the answer. Perhaps Mr. John Morley will by-and-by be so good as to favour me with it, in the interests of truth and science.

OFFERING AND SACRIFICE.

say, then they would have been far better employed than in running, like those who neglect the keeping of their own house clean, to the " wise and ancient " Pope of Rome, to seek recognition of Anglican Orders, which can be procured with no knowledge whatever of Hebrew, and but a shaky—very shaky—knowledge of Greek, and to get a thoroughgoing snub too. And yet these ill-educated, and wholly self-conscious, superior persons, many ordained Anglican clergymen, look down on men in every respect their betters and fitted in every way to be their teachers, even in essentials. And on their behalf men go running to the Pope to help them to be yet more arrogant and pretentious. Let the great Temple of Canterbury, as a true Lessingite, stir them up.

PART III.

THE MAZZOTH OR PASSOVER.

III.

The Mazzoth, or the Passover of the Hebrews, was the Spring festival, as the Feast of Harvest or of Weeks was the Summer one, and the Feast of Ingathering was the Autumn festival. But these feasts were in no sense strictly confined to the Hebrew people, for most nations in their earlier stages have been naturally led to keep the same seasons as being of special solemnity or rejoicing, and more particularly the first and third. Bishop Colenso found these, or something closely corresponding to them, among the Zulus, and more especially, as he says, this applies to the *ukwetzama*. The time of the celebration of the Passover lay between March 20th and April 23rd, and there was to be offered on this occasion

OFFERING AND SACRIFICE.

"a sheaf of the first fruits of barley-harvest," barley-harvest being thus early in Palestine.

Pesach was the eve of the full moon of that month, and among all Eastern nations, and indeed some not Eastern, that full moon had especial significance. Some writers have presented various considerations leading them to question whether the Jews did not get the idea from some other people rather than initiate the thing themselves; and, whatever may be said as to that, inquiry does sow doubts—serious doubts—whether it was initiated at the time of Moses at all, or indeed needed any such institution. One of the most extraordinary facts about it is that the Passover itself is not even once named by any one of the Scripture historians, psalmists, and prophets before the Captivity, except only in the case of Josiah's Passover, 2 Kings xxiii. 21 [1] (see Colenso vi. p. 178), and that surely looks rather queer, since we know

---

[1] "Surely there was not holden such a passover from the days of the judges that judged Israel, nor in all the

PESACH = PASSING OVER.

so well that long before that there were so many passings-over to Jahvé.

Colenso may well write:

"When we take all the above facts into consideration, it seems highly probable that the Pesach meant originally the 'passing-over' of the firstborns of man and beast to the Sun-god, and that the Canaanites—*i.e.*, the Phœnicians and others—did actually at this Spring festival, on the 14th day of the month, *i.e.*, the eve of the full moon, sacrifice their firstborns to that deity, from whom the Israelites adopted the practice of sacrificing their firstborns to Jehovah (Yahwé)."[1]

Surely another thing much against the whole claim put forward for the Hebrew festivals as set down especially in Deuteronomy is this, that the Pesach, which was said to have been originated in Egypt, as well as the feast of unleavened bread,

days of the kings of Israel, nor of the kings of Judah;" and we simply say, very significant indeed from our point of view. No passover, though many passings-over.

"Pentateuch," vi. p. 430.

OFFERING AND SACRIFICE.

cannot be traced back so far as the feast of tents or tabernacles any more than the harvest festival or feast of weeks. These latter are distinctly agricultural festivals, as the Pesach is a pastoral one strictly, and could neither have had origination in Egypt nor during the wanderings, nor till a complete settlement was made in Canaan.

As, however, we find the word הַעֲבִיר, *passing-over*, and derivates from it, both nouns and parts of verbs, used so often in this sense, as in Exod. xiii. 12, "Thou shalt make them *pass over* to Jehovah," what is so very absurd in supposing that, if they did not absolutely originate the practice, they were in early days so persistent in it that they took the name Hebrews (Passers-over) from it—the people pre-eminently that in those early days made their sons to *pass over* to their Sun-god? These phenomena entirely agree with our view that, not to speak of the earlier times, even so late as the days of Jeremiah and Ezekiel no such redemption-

BEYOND JORDAN.

money as is indicated in the Levitical Code was ever paid, but the firstborns of men, if dedicated at all, were simply sacrificed, and the people quoted the old laws as enjoining the practice.[1] עִבְרִים indeed!

At Exodus xii. 11, for the "Lord's Passover" we have פֶּסַח לַיהוָה; but the very first words of the next sentence recall us to our position. Jahvé says: "And I will pass over [or through] the land of Egypt," and the Hebrew is וְעָבַרְתִּי בְאֶרֶץ־מִצְרַיִם. Their god himself was the first passer-over: here, as elsewhere, they but followed where he himself showed the way.

There is one case where the Authorised English translators do not wish them, even in their own sense and that of their language, to be really Hebrews, Passers-over. That is at Deut. i. 1, where it is clear the Hebrew means "beyond Jordan," but the Authorised translators make it "on this side." בְּעֵבֶר הַיַּרְדֵּן most certainly cannot be twisted to mean "on this side."

[1] "Pentateuch," vi. p. 431.

OFFERING AND SACRIFICE.

As even Bleek says: "It is against the usages of the language," and that utterly.

The form given above was an established equivalent for the country lying eastwards of the Jordan, without any reference to the place where the person writing it may have been. Nor can it be correct, in the one case, to write, "Beyond Jordan in the land of Moab," or, in the other, "on this side Jordan in the land of Moab," as it is at verse 5. Beyond Jordan there clearly means to the west of it, in the sense of having passed over it, and here, as elsewhere, there are doubts and doubles about the *passing-over* in this sense; so that the Hebrews to the east of Jordan were Hebrews, but not passers-over in that sense, and yet passers-over.

Then, again, if it is, as Bleek says, the form given above was an established equivalent for the country lying eastwards of Jordan, how comes it that at v. 25 of 3rd chapter we have from Moses himself: "I pray thee, let me go over (אֶעְבְּרָה־נָּא) and see the good land that is beyond

AN INCONSISTENCY

the Jordan (הַיַּרְדֵּן בְּעֵבֶר), that goodly mountain [or rather mountainous land] and Lebanon"? That most clearly is spoken by one still in the east of Jordan, speaking of the land to the west of it, who had not yet, at all events in the permanent sense, passed over, as he clearly longed and aspired to do.

And what is really the ground for saying that the Hebrews learned the bloody practice of passing-over from the Canaanites? It is exceedingly funny—nothing less—to see how fond and anxious able and disinterested critics are to find excuses for the Hebrews (Passers-over) in the example of others—others, by the way, whom they despised and hated, and certainly did not, anyway, look up to, so as to run and imitate them in such matters.[1] But there is here really no

---

[1] Prior to the Captivity, the besetting sin of the Jews was their proneness to polytheism and idolatry, *caused by their intercourse with heathen neighbours*, which inclination prompted and commerce necessitated.* What an

* "Spectator," August 15, 1896.

OFFERING AND SACRIFICE.

ground at all—not a bit—because in their very language we have the proof of it, as we have of so many other things. Their ceremonial Pesach or Passover was the very clumsiest invention to account for, and in a way to justify, their long-continued and inveterate practice of passing over, and with a most ingenious play on the word, too—a practice so long continued that even Abraham's offering up of Isaac is a mere modified survival of it. That is, if for the moment you put criticism aside and regard the offering of Isaac as anything else than mythical. assumption have we here, and what a contradiction!—(1) assumption that the Jews were polytheistic only through intercourse with heathens—"*caused* by their intercourse with heathens"; and (2) while this is so, there are the promptings of inclination and necessitations of commerce. But why this kind of trimming, this nonsensical see-sawing? In no period of their history were they, according to their own account, more prone to idolatry than they were in the wilderness wanderings—setting up the golden calf; with tents or tabernacles of Moloch and Chiun (Saturn), their idols, the star of their Elohim, etc., etc. Now, in the desert it surely cannot be said that they were in contact with heathen neighbours in any way, to tempt or to aid and abet them in their proneness to polytheism. And we have no ground for thinking that this asserted forty years' discipline cured them, have we?

OFFERING OF ISAAC.

We do not. There are the very best grounds for holding that the account of Abraham's intended sacrifice of Isaac in Gen. xxii. was written in David's age, with a view, indeed, of discouraging the practice, but yet *commending* it, as emanating from a holy and Divine impulse, and certainty not condemning it.[1]

This is a most important point, as proving by another class of evidence that in the time of David human sacrifices and "passings through the fire" were common, so as to call for this kind at once of indirect justification, apology, and commendation of substitution. Colenso may therefore well say: "It is possible that circumcision may have had as its origin a religious meaning, expressing the dedication of all males to Jehovah by the sacrifice of a part for the whole."[2] As we find this process universal, from the fact to the fiction, from real observance to ceremonial, why

---

[1] Colenso, Oort, p. 24.
[2] "Pentateuch," vi. p. 415 (note).

OFFERING AND SACRIFICE.

draw back and decline to draw the proper inference here?

That suggests going back a long way, for the observance, of which circumcision is but the ceremonial symbol, goes back far beyond Abraham. The sign of admission into the covenant of Jahvé is specifically circumcision. Even the stranger may thus qualify. The stranger who resides (to be, however, well distinguished from the day hireling merely passing through or sojourning for a time, Exod. xii. 45—47) may be admitted to partake of the Passover with his family if all his males are first circumcised (Exod. xii. 44; comp. Gen. xvii. 12, 13, 27, 48). Over and over again we have the words, "No uncircumcised person shall eat thereof (Exod. xii. 48). "My covenant shall be in your flesh an everlasting covenant" (Gen. xvii. 13). "And the uncircumcised man-child, whose flesh of his foreskin is not circumcised, that soul shall be cut off from his people;" which, let it be borne in mind, is precisely the same doom as being imperfect or having been acciden-

CIRCUMCISION AND PASSOVER.

tally injured there—for every one that was so was cut off from the congregation! And then there is the resemblance which Kuenen notices between the law of the Passover in Exod. xii. 1—18, 40—51, and the law of circumcision in Gen. xvii. In language and in manner he says that they entirely agree.

Now, what on earth could be the reason of this? Why was circumcision so absolutely linked with the Passover, and why were strangers and their whole families, if circumcised, admitted to it? These questions I leave for others to answer, reserving in the meantime my own thoughts about them. Only this will I say, that as the Philistines were the only people near to the Hebrews in Palestine that did not practise circumcision, it is very hard to see how this mere circumcision could for the strangers be made an effective term of communion, as we might put it, for sharing in the Passover, unless indeed the Passover might be taken to mean the passing-over, as we have hinted

OFFERING AND SACRIFICE.

it was—a thing the stranger might very well understand and believe in as not being so very remote from his own practice and ideal: only the difficulty emerges that there would be few of them that had not already undergone the rite. The intention, however, is clear, that if they were willing even to undergo it they ceremonially subscribed to what it signified —the passing-over. The same fact, and the circle of facts which it suggests, militate against our subscribing fully to Mr. Herbert Spencer's theory of trophies.

And if thus there was the passing-over, there was the passing-over eating, which, in the sense we here mean, was, as we have seen it in so many other cases, veritably a god-eating.

PART IV.

FURTHER CORROBORATIONS.

IV.

I.

By the very act of sacrifice the animal or human victim was thus supposed to be blended with the deity, if not actually identified with him. This underlies the whole process. We have seen it clearly in the case of the Khonds. It was not otherwise in the case of the Hindoos, nor of the Greeks, as Dr. F. Granger tells. Here are the words of Siva, given in extract from the " Calica Purana ":

" When this has been done, O my children " (that is, the preparation and sanctification of the victim), " the victim is even as myself, and the guardian deities of the ten quarters take up abode in him. Then Brâhma and all the other deities assemble together in the victim, and, be

OFFERING AND SACRIFICE.

he ever so much a sinner, he is made free from sin; and then his pure blood changes to Ambrosia, and he gains the love of Mahadevi, the goddess of Yog-Niddra (*i.e.*, complete repose and tranquillity of mind), the goddess of the whole universe, or rather the universe itself." [1]

Nor was it, if we have read the records aright, in any respect different with the Hebrews. No one denies that in earlier times human sacrifices were offered in Israel.

"It is true human sacrifice was no uncommon thing in those days, and there is reason to fear that the Israelites did not keep themselves pure from the unnatural worship of Moloch." [2]

So Dr. Marcus Dods, who is still a minister of the Free Church of Scotland, and a most respected and influential one. But he qualifies rather too much, though by no means do we accuse him of throwing dust up and under cover of it playing

[1] "Asiatic Researches," v. p. 379.
[2] "Israel's Iron Age," p. 164.

THE REDEMPTION CLAUSE.

thimble-rig with names—names such as Ba'al, Moloch, Jahvé—as some do. But it remains to ask, what about the lots of men hung up before Jahvé? what about the holocausts of enemies offered to Jahvé? what about the many, many passings-over to Jahvé?

And as to the redemption clause at Lev. xiii. 15, it is clearly an interpolation of later times, directly inconsistent with definite legislation elsewhere, and making much else in the Pentateuch—not to speak of writings of the prophets—utterly unmeaning. Let us look to this a little more particularly, and in the course of our inquiries we shall see that not only were the Hebrews, like most other early races, guilty of human sacrifice, but that they were cannibals, and that the Meriah sacrifices were hardly more dreadful than what was customary with them.

We are clearly told that Ahaz and Manasseh " burned their sons in the fire," and that the great majority of the Hebrew monarchs followed "the evil example of

OFFERING AND SACRIFICE.

their fathers." It may well be asked, what could have been the practices of these fathers prior to the admonitions and protests of prophets, or when the prophets themselves scarcely censured, if by silence they did not approve, or still more when men like Samuel and Elijah and David—the highly-cultivated man and "full flower of monotheism," as Dr. Fairbairn has most eloquently said— themselves killed and offered up men as a sacrificial rite?

Jehu, we read, served the Lord and destroyed Ba'al and the priests of Ba'al by a stratagem, and yet he sacrificed to the golden calves (bulls) that were in Dan and Bethel, and we know all too well what that implies—the offering of the firstborn. Here we have the dreadful observance on the part of an enemy of Ba'al and the priests of Ba'al.[1]

And how utterly inconsistent, how utterly absurd, it is to represent that because as asserted the firstborn of Egypt

---

[1] 1 Kings xii. 28, and 2 Kings x. 18.

THE LEVITES.

were slain by the angel of God, while Hebrew firstborns were passed over, the firstborn of Israel should in after ages be offered in celebration of this—that the Passover should be remembered by such a hideous rite! No; the Passover is, in our idea, a mere invention, a mere myth, framed, clumsily framed, in after times to account for and to give a *kind* of *raison d'être* for the practice of human sacrifice and its accompaniments, traces of which all too clearly remained in the Hebrew ritual as in the Hebrew Scriptures.

It was in Solomon's time that the ecclesiastical system of the nation was first concentrated, by one only place of legitimate worship—Jerusalem and its temple—being now appointed, and one high priest only permitted. Until this time the Levites seem to have been no organised body, and to have exercised no appreciable religious, or even ritual, influence over the nation. And until now, and for long after this, there was no priestly instruction, no circulation of the

OFFERING AND SACRIFICE.

Scriptures, no general education, no observance of the Sabbatical year, it may be, and none of the year of jubilee; and there was image-worship to an extent which it is difficult for us to calculate or to comprehend. We can find no trace of the celebration of the Passover between the time of Moses and of Josiah, and none of the Feast of Tabernacles before the Captivity; and it is said, speaking of an observance of this after their return, "Since the days of Joshua the son of Nun unto that day, had not the children of Israel done so." These things surely indicate an imperfection in the religious and civil constitutions of the Jewish people, and that for more than half the whole period of their national existence, which we never could have anticipated from a mere knowledge of the aim of their election, and which contradicts all that we should have anticipated from the whole tone of the Mosaic law.[1]

It is, then, nothing more than a fair

[1] Myers, "Catholic Thoughts on the Bible," p 314

inference, and judging from what we find elsewhere, that the Passover was a later invention, got up to take the place of human sacrifices, and to justify, most inconsistently however, their way of observing what was really a universal custom or rite.

Bleek is very anxious to show how, even among the kings whose zeal to promote the true worship of Jehovah was most undoubted—*Asa, Jehoshaphat, Joash, Amaziah, Uzziah*—the practice of offering on other places than before the Ark obtained; and he goes on to say:

" In the Books of Kings and Chronicles it is always pointed out as *blamable* that even these pious kings should have allowed the worship in high places to remain. But this is no more than the verdict of the writer of these books, which in no case could have been composed before the Babylonian exile. As the kings above named are depicted in everything else as such zealous servants of Jehovah, we can scarcely think that they would not have aimed at putting a stop to the worship at high places, where sacrifices were offered to Jehovah at other altars besides in the Temple, if the Deuteronomic law, so expressly showing this service to be contrary to the will of Jehovah, had been known to and acknowledged by them as Mosaic. . . . The Deuteronomic legislation was not composed by the same author whom we have before us in the middle books of the Pentateuch, and was composed at a considerably later time than that to which, in all probability, we should assign the Jehovistic revision of the ancient Israelitish history and Mosaic lawgiving as we now have it in the preceding books of the Pentateuch."[1]

It is further pointed out by Bleek that, notwithstanding the Deuteronomic direction that there should be but one place of offering or oblation (the sanctuary where the Ark was), the sanctuary was not treated as fixed at the seat of the Ark, but in many places—high places and all the rest of it;

[1] I. pp. 327, 328.

A CRASS INVENTION.

and, in truth, there never was any strict observance of this direction—none at all—as the rites of Bethel and Dan too openly show. There was not even the effort to observe, nor is there over the larger space of the history any the least sense of a wrong done to Jahvé in so acting towards him; the clear inference being that the Levitical code was not then in existence any more than the Deuteronomic, which, however, was later, as is proved by the fact that it tries to accommodate here.

And one further inference forced on the careful reader by all this is that the Levites is clearly an invention of later days to account for certain influences and symbols not mentioned by earlier prophets. The earliest prophets who speak of them are Jeremiah (xxxiii. 8) and Ezekiel (xl. 46, xlviii. 11).

In truth, the usual orthodox representation will not bear looking at. It, like the thing it deals with, is a crass invention, if not imposture, meant to keep people in ignorance and in submission to a priestly

OFFERING AND SACRIFICE.

caste, as the good Mr. Samuel Sharpe himself said:

"The ceremonial laws, while attempting to regulate the religious practices then thought useful, show a strong priestly wish to bring the people into a state of ignorant obedience to their religious leaders. Even the moral laws are often directed to the same selfish end; and there were few crimes from which a man might not fancy himself relieved by an offering to the priest and the altar." ("History of Hebrew People," p. 105.)

And to see how real a matter th redeeming of the firstborn was, one has only to read the last section (v. 44—51) of the third chapter of Numbers. The sons referred to in Exod. xxii. 29, could not be meant for the service of the Temple, because every required service was otherwise provided for. Everything which was said in Sacred Writ to be devoted to the Lord, by the original meaning of the word "devoted" (though the word became in time changed), was meant to be sacrificed.

VON BOHLEN.

The change was due to a wish of the priest to appropriate the devoted article to his own use instead of burning it.[1]

Von Bohlen and many others following him find that the Passover on the 15th day of the month Nisan [the month of April] is simply the *fête* of the Spring-time, of the Sun-god;[2] and he, as well as Ewerbeck and Ghillany, holds that two reminiscences of these human sacrifices remain in (1) the universal prostitution to the deity in the East—that is, the offering of the virginity instead of the life; and, on the male side, the offering of the foreskins in circumcision to the god, and indirectly, for the god, to the king as his high priest. Ghillany holds that the myth of Cronos devouring his own children is th latest *souvenir* of this almost universal sacrifice of children. "It remained," he

[1] Higgins, "Celtic Druids," pp. 292, 293.
[2] "Comme von Bohlen, je crois que le passah, *les pâques*, était d'abord une fête de printemps, du dieu Soleil, et en même temps de la moisson qui a lieu dans ce climat chaud au mois d'Avril (15 du mois Nisan, commencement de l'année)." (Ghillany, "Sacrifices Humains chez les Hebreux," ii. 317.)

OFFERING AND SACRIFICE.

adds, "the true national cult of the Hebrews, and was at its height in the period from Solomon to Zedekiah."[1]

One of the main accompaniments of sacrifice was eating of the offering.

II.

It was an essential part of the sacrificial service, indeed, that what was offered unto God should be shared by men—by those who worshipped and offered. If, therefore, there were human sacrifices, the Hebrews were cannibals, as they had a cannibal god in Jahvé. Nor is the point

[1] "En Chypres, d'après Justin, le sacrifice de la vie humaine fut remplacé entièrement par celui de la virginité. Même dans la Grèce continentale les Locriens assiégés par Lycophron le despote, promettent à Vénus de lui faire immoler la virginité de toutes les vierges locrinnes quand Lycophron aura été butta. La déesse Anaïte en Perse de même (Klinker, Append. au Zendavesta, iii. 61): bref, la prostitution en l'honneur de la divinité était à l'ordre du jour chez tous les Orientaux." (*Ibid.* ii. p. 229.)

"La circoncision n'abolit pas cependant les sacrifices humains tout à fait : elle les restreignit à quelques cas solés, mais solennellement périodiques." (*Ibid.* ii. p. 240.)

EZEKIEL.

left merely to inference. Ezekiel is full of it—the horror of it literally possesses him.[1] His book is red with blood as the land was, according to him—of human blood, of the blood of children sacrificed. Read the 9th, 16th, 18th, 20th, 23rd, 33rd, and 36th chapters, more especially the 13th and 18th verses of this last chapter. The translators have done their level best to hide the enormities of it, but the truth —the dreadful truth—they could not hide. Isaiah bursts forth now and then to the same effect as Ezekiel: " Enflaming yourselves with idols under every green tree, slaying the children in the valley, under the clifts of the rocks " (lvii. 5). Turn now to a typical passage in Ezekiel (xvi. 20, 21):

" Thou hast taken thy sons and thy daughters, whom thou hast borne unto me, and these hast thou sacrificed unto them to [devour] be devoured. . . . Thou hast slain my children, and delivered them to cause them to pass through the fire for them."

[1] Read also Jer. vii. 31 ; xix. 4 ; xxxii. 35.

OFFERING AND SACRIFICE.

Again, take this:

"Because men say of thee that thou art a man-eater (אֹכֶלֶת אָדָם אָתִּי), and hast made thy people childless; therefore thou shalt no more eat men, nor be cannibal to thy children: I will no more hear the reproach of thee among the heathen" (Ezek. xxxvi. 13).

And here, most assuredly, we have one of the funniest perversions for a purpose by translation ever effected on any book. The translators in first clause translated by us insert the word "land"—"thou *and*"—where in the original there is no suggestion of *land* in any form; and in some editions with marginal references a reference is given to Numbers xiii. 32, where the spies report on the land as eating up men! But a change of subject is indicated clearly in the Hebrew here by the space or sign of new paragraph—which is more marked indeed than it is even at v. 16—and to this the translators pay no heed whatever. In truth, the change from apostrophising the land to addressing

REVISED TRANSLATION.

the people begins at v. 13, and not at v. 16, as the Authorised Version would fain make out; and the connection of ideas with v. 17 is clear: "When the house of Israel abode in their own land, they defiled it by their own way and by their doings: their way was before my face as the uncleanness of a woman removed. Wherefore I poured my fury upon them for *the blood that they had shed upon the land*" (it was in this sense the land figurately *ate men*), "*and for their idols with which they had polluted it.* Therefore I scattered them among the heathen." As though the land was blighted and barren because of the curse brought on it by their uncleanness and idolatry. The word for "idols" here, by-the-bye, is גלולים— —the essential idea of which is something round—that is, pillar or pole or *ashera*. To our mind there is no suggestion in the Hebrew to justify the reference to Numbers, which is most literally: "Thou shalt not eat men any more, nor be any more cannibal of thy corpses [or bodies]."

The Revised Translation, sad to say,

OFFERING AND SACRIFICE.

here follows and perpetuates the blunders of the Authorised Version, which is not to be wondered at, perhaps, in a body that could change "Unstable as water, thou shalt not excel," into "Thou shalt not attain unto any excellency." They make uncalled-for alterations and spoil the English; where very serious alterations were wanted, they simply let things slide or trim and half-do, like the busybodies that they were, one and all of them.

All this is splendidly illustrated at Psalm cx. 6, where we have יָדִין בַּגּוֹיִם (he shall judge among the heathen), and then מָלֵא גְוִיּוֹת (he shall fill with the dead bodies).[1]

Jeremiah is quite as definite and as

[1] In unpointed Hebrew the plurals of the words גְוִיָּה and גּוֹיִם would be very like each other, though גּוֹיִם could hardly be mistaken for גְּוִיּוֹת, and certainly גּוֹיִם (bodies), *pointed*, which is identical with גּוֹיִם (peoples, nations, bodies corporate), might very easily be confounded; while, in pointing various forms of the words afterwards, mistakes might very easily have arisen—not to speak of mistakes in translation—in part, at all events, dictated by preconceptions. (Myers' idea of Christianising Mosaism largely to blame; see "Catholic Thoughts.")

PSALM CVI.

insistent. He cries out: "They have built the high places of Baal, *to burn their sons with fire for burnt offerings* unto Baal, which I commanded them not" (xx. 5). Here be it noticed they are not burnt *in* the fire, so that any cover could be given to a mere ceremonial passing or leaping through flames, but *burned with fire* and *for burnt offerings*. If there is any loophole here for Mr. Lang to cleverly creep through, we cannot see it.

And once more: "They have committed adultery, and blood is on their hands; with their idols they have committed adultery, and have also caused their sons, whom they bare unto me, to be passed through the fire and *given them for food*" (xxiii. 37).[1]

And if any doubt can still remain, surely this unexpected utterance, or series of remarkable utterances, in that altogether noteworthy Psalm cvi. would settle it. Listen: "They joined themselves unto

[1] Read also especially, with close care, Numbers xiv. 9; Isa. lvii. 5; lix. 3; Ezek. xviii. 6, 11, and 15; xxii. 3; xxxiii. 25; xxxvi. 18; Zech. ix. 15; Hosea ii. 11, 12, 16, 17.

OFFERING AND SACRIFICE.

Baal-Peor, *and ate the sacrifices of the dead*" (v. 28). "And they served their idols which were a shame unto them. Yea, they sacrificed their sons and their daughters unto the demons [devils]. And shed innocent blood, even the blood of their sons and of their daughters, whom they sacrificed unto the idols of Canaan: and the land was polluted with blood" (vv. 37, 38).

This is but a kind of poetical rendering of Numbers xxv. 2, 3:

"And they called the people unto the sacrifices of their gods, and the people did eat"—[What? The Psalm above is absolutely clear what it was]—"and bowed down to their gods.

"And Israel joined himself unto Baal-Peor."[1]

And the words of the Psalm are a very faithful rendering of the Hebrew, as faithful as we find anywhere.

And every Hebrew scholar knows well what פְּעוֹר means, פְּעוֹר, of which בַּעַל is lord or master, just as Siva = Arganatha is lord of the boat-shaped vessel =

DR. PEROWNE.

It is funny—nothing short of funny—to read the comments of men like Dr. Perowne, now Bishop of Worcester, on such clauses as this.[1] He would fain explain it away, and suggests by apt quotation from others that by the dead may be meant "idols," as opposed to the "living God," and says, as an alternative reading, that it may mean necromantic rites, as of "one seeking to the dead." But seeking to the dead is wholly different; here the plain word in Hebrew is אָכְלוּ, ate, and the word for "dead" is clear—מֵתִים, dead bodies. Bishop Perowne is ingenious, he is very clever, almost to the point of succeeding, but this will not do; and he would have to face and to explain away in quite a different style from what he has yet done the grounds

---

Yoni; it is = Peorapis = Priapus: and the rites associated with the worship all round were beastly. The inclination of the Jews for this is enough to prove that either all the claims they made for special revelation to them are lies, or that they were so foul as to wallow in this filth after light had been fully revealed to them. Either they lie, or they were so low and contemptibly filthy as to take no benefit from such wonderful revelations as were made to them.

[1] Perowne, "Psalms," ii. p. 255.

OFFERING AND SACRIFICE.

for the oft-repeated denunciations of eating things offered to idols. This ingenious effort of Bishop Perowne is like so much else: it half-shies looking at plain words, and would make Hebrew metaphorical in a sense it never really was. We do not expect much light on such matters from such an exercise as Mr. Richard Holt Hutton's fine, fine essay on Hebrew poetry, nor do we get it.

Unfortunately for Dr. Perowne and those whom he cites, all fain to give a kind of countenance to the idea that the plain word מֵתִים here meant idols, a wholly different word, and the proper one is given at v. 36; it is עֲצַבַּת, idol.

When Hupfeld objects that in Numbers xxv. 2 the same sacrifices are called "sacrifices of their gods," and that sacrifices to the dead would scarcely be accompanied by sacrificial feasts, Dr. Perowne is surely right in urging that this last objection has no force. But the Hebrew is clear: it is not "ate sacrifices to the

ONLY DESTINATION WRONG.

dead," but "ate sacrifices of the dead"— a very different matter.

There can be no question that to sacrifice here means to slaughter, and, to leave no doubt, the word slaughter itself is used; and also the actual and common word for eating is used—a word about which no Hebrew scholar can be in the least in doubt.

It is the same word (הֶעֱבִיר) which is used in the expression to pass over children to Moloch, as is used in the passage already quoted from Leviticus, to pass over to Jahvé; so that if the children of Israel passed their children through the fire to Moloch, it was the destination that was wrong, and not the process; for they were directed in the Levitical law, by the self-same word, to pass them over in the same way to Jahvé. וַיַּעֲבִירוּ is the first word used in the 17th verse of 2 Kings xvii. It is the same word that is used in the close of v. 10 of 2 Kings xxiii., in the clause "to pass through the fire to Moloch."

And the sacrifice of Saul's seven

OFFERING AND SACRIFICE.

sons (grandsons) by David through the Gibeonites, be it noted, took place, of all possible times, at the beginning of barley harvest, which was, of course, the time of the Passover feast. Even the exceedingly cautious Samuel Sharpe, referring to Manasseh's passing his son through the fire, speaks of it as a superstitious ceremony which was *often* used as a cover for infanticide (p. 139).

But look what the more critical Canon Venables has written—his words afford little support to the idea that Hebrew "passings through the fire" were "harmless rites," as Mr. Andrew Lang boldly suggests:

"The fiendish custom of infant sacrifice to the fire-gods seems to have been kept up in Tophet, at its S.E. extremity, for a considerable period. To put an end to these abominations, the place was polluted by Josiah, who rendered it ceremonially unclean by spreading over it human bones and other corruptions, from which time it appears to have become the common

ISAIAH.

cesspool of the city, into which its sewage was conducted, to be carried off by the waters of the Kedron. Robinson declares 'there is no evidence of any other fires than those of Moloch having ever been kept up in this valley.' From its ceremonial defilement, and from the detested and abominable fire of Moloch, . . . the latter Jews applied the name of this valley, *Ge Hinnom*—*Gehenna*—to denote the place of eternal torment, and some of the Rabbis here fixed 'the door of hell'— a sense in which it is used by our Lord." (G. Venables, M.A.)

III.

Before you have got over the first twenty verses of Isaiah he is on the same key, denouncing thus: " Your hands are full of blood" (i. 15); and the second Isaiah, or another, passes on to the very same key again at chap. lix. 3: "Your hands are defiled with blood, and your fingers with

OFFERING AND SACRIFICE.

iniquity"; and again at v. 6: "Your works are works of iniquity, and the act of violence is in your hands; your feet run to evil, and they make haste to shed innocent blood." In a condition where sacrifice was the rule, was this in the least likely to arise as the protest of prophets with regard to *that*—the killing of animals? Not at all. The smell of the sacrifice was in their minds, as God said it was in His, sweet. It was human blood only which could be to them in such light that they could speak thus of it. And not only that. The Hebrews regarded foreign enemies as mere animals for sacrifice, and the prophetical writings bear abundant witness to this as well as do the words of Balaam: "Behold, the people shall rise up as a lion, as a young lion; he shall not lie down till he eat the prey, and drink the blood of the slain. He shall eat up his enemies, and gnaw their bones." This was essentially the Hebrew idea of those outside their circle, and in the spirit of this they consistently and constantly acted.

INNOCENT BLOOD.

The innocent blood, therefore, could only apply to blood of their own kin—to blood of children especially killed, offered in sacrifice and eaten, or partially eaten, as sacrifices invariably were.

Now, the orthodox theologian thinks he gets a rise out of us by urging that the prophets were protestors on behalf of Jahvé against Ba'al and Moloch; but we have to remind him of hundreds on hundreds "hung up" in the sun before their own Jahvé—only another kind of passing through the fire—have to point to the law of the firstborn, clearly enough laid down in their own records, though attempts have been made to work it out by substitutions and redeemings.

When Zechariah (ix. 15) describes the victorious Jews, under guidance of Jahvé, as eating their enemies' flesh and drinking their blood as it were with the riot and relish of winebibbers, nay, as gorging themselves with blood, not only like the vessels filled within, but like the corners of the altar gory without, it might at first

OFFERING AND SACRIFICE.

sight be supposed that the description is a rhetorical figure; but, when we learn from history that the very same atrocities were literally enacted against their fellow-colonists by the Jews of Cyrene, some of whom were probably descended from ancestors who left Palestine before the improvements in the law introduced by Ezra and Nehemiah, and who, as we know from Jeremiah, had never been favourable to reform, it becomes exceedingly probable that these excesses were not unprecedented, but that, as the realisation of the prophecy was a fanatical outbreak of ancient barbarism, so the prophecy itself was conceived from the possible recurrence of habits not yet forgotten or obsolete.[1]

We have truly some very ghastly records of wholesale wanton and bloody slaughter, if the element of sacrifice did not come in. There is the slaughter of the more than four hundred priests of Baal by Elijah (who, by the way, became quite Jack and Tom with worshippers of Ba'al at Sarepta)

Mackay, ii. p. 413.

THE SACRIFICIAL ELEMENT.

there is the slaughter of the prophets of Ba'al by Jehu;[1] there is again the murder by Jehu of Ahab's seventy children, whose heads, we are told, were heaped up at either side of the entrance of the gate of the city. That is significant; what became of the bodies? They could not very well have been a sacrifice to Ba'al. Was there anything sacrificial in these holocausts? The sacrificial element alone relieves the horror, only, however, to add a fresh and different horror—the eating of human flesh —but that, if we read hundreds of passages in the prophets and elsewhere that will not really bear a mere metaphorical interpretation, was common with the Israelites.

Beltane fires, on the 1st of May, are still kept up in the Isle of Man (see Train's "Isle of Man," i. p. 328), as well as in some remote parts of Scotland; and these suffice to tell that even in these northern regions human sacrifices and similar observances took place at the same season of the year.

[1] 2 Kings x. 18—28.

OFFERING AND SACRIFICE.

In the "Statistical Account of Scotland" the clergyman of the parish of Callander tells that it was customary for the people to assemble on the moor, round a fire, where, he says, "they bake a cake, which they divide into as many portions, as similar as possible to one another in size and shape, as there are persons in the company. They daub one of these portions all over with charcoal, until it be perfectly black. They put all the bits of the cake into a bonnet. Every one, blindfolded, draws out a portion, and he who holds the bonnet is entitled to the last bit. Whoever draws the black bit is the devoted person who is to be sacrificed to *Baal* (or Bel), whose favour they mean to implore, in rendering the year productive of the sustenance of man and beast. There is little doubt of these inhuman human sacrifices having been once offered *in this country*, as well as in the East, although they now pass from the act of sacrificing, and only compel the devoted person to leap three times through the flames, with which

THE DEVOTED PERSON.

the ceremonies of the festival are closed."[1]

The cake baked at the open fire on the moor, and divided into as many portions as there were persons present, is clearly identical with the unleavened bread of the Passover of the Jews; the charcoal daub is a substitute for blood—for human blood—as we have found it at pp. 23 and 49; and we have here clearly a survival of an observance which was common to Phœnicia, to Israel, to Syria, and other places at certain times and periods. Very wonderful and suggestive to find illustrations and survivals of old Eastern Ba'al rites at our own doors. Here there is no priest—that office is performed by those present. So in Israel: each head of a household could kill the Passover, and the qualification of the whole nation as "holy" (Exod. xix. 6) most probably alludes to the ancient universality of priestly privileges.

We are wholly at one with a reliable writer when he deliberately says:

[1] Vol. ii. p. 62.

OFFERING AND SACRIFICE.

"The new Passover replaced the old Moloch rite, in which, if analogy may be a basis for conjecture, a man or a child was hung, or rather crucified, as an offering 'before the Lord' (that is Jahvé), during the last hours of the departing year; and, after being suspended till sunset, was then taken down, the blood poured out upon unleavened cakes, which, with portions of the flesh, were eaten by the communicants, and the remains burnt in the furnace fire of Moloch, the still-continuing title of Jehovah in Paschal invocations."

Mackay well points out that the Passover was the solar festival common to all nations, particularly to the Phœnicians and their colonies—at the commencement of the year (that is, the springtime), when the Egyptians, and even the Peruvians, smeared their doors, their sheep, or their fruit trees with blood.[1]

The Levitical law allowed no killing of animals save in sacrifice; all had, *under pain of death*, to be brought and killed

[1] Vol. i. p. 448.

BLOOD POURED OUT.

before the door of the sanctuary. The Levitical code, in fact, forbade the eating of flesh unless sanctified; the Deuteronomic code, as Bleek well points out, "as if partly in opposition to the above law, expressly permits that (except for sacrifices) the Israelites might slay beasts and eat their flesh after their desire, according to the blessing of Jehovah their God; only they were to refrain from consuming the blood, and were to pour it out on the earth like water; whilst, according to Leviticus xvii. 6, the blood was always to be brought to the priest, and was to be sprinkled before the tabernacle."[1]

Now, the utter and conclusive absurdity of this law is that it is absolutely and physically unworkable. It was professedly legislated at a time when the idea of one temple for the whole kingdom — thus securing unity by annihilation of distance! — was also introduced; and just as Dr. Colenso has proved — and unanswerably proved — that it was, on account of rivers,

[1] Vol. i. p. 326.

OFFERING AND SACRIFICE.

rains, &c., absolutely impossible that the people should have twice a year—not to speak of thrice a year—gone up to Jerusalem, so it is impossible, for similar good reasons, that the people could have observed this law, let them try ever so.

If in the time of the Captivity the Israelites mixed up cannibalism with their idolatry, as there is and can be no doubt they did, it becomes only too clear that their scribes, fain to throw a glamour over the past, or, as the critics say, to improve the original picture in painting over it, did, quite consciously, read the feelings of a later age into an earlier one, whether for edification or not, and made, so far as they could, a wholly false report. If such things were done in the time of Ezekiel, what, we ask again, must have been the condition of matters when, as we are told was the case in the time of the Judges, "every man did that which was right in his own eyes"?

How much, says Pliny, do we owe to Roman civilisation for abolishing the horrible superstition which made the killing

MERIAH SACRIFICES.

of a man a most pious act, and the eating of him a most healthy and nourishing one!

Thus human sacrifice among the Hebrews, as among the Khonds of Orissa and other peoples, was simply a god-eating and a god-drinking. If it was not this, then it was something worse than this—yet worse and more savage than this. Only such an idea, perverted though it may be, can redeem it from the lowest and basest savagery; only by allowing this idea to enter into it do you raise it even to the level of the Meriah sacrifice. If you will not admit this idea, then Hebrew sacrifice, and the partaking of human sacrifices, reduces them wholly to the low level of the lowest cannibal negroes.

The cannibals of the Congo are perhaps the most thorough-going of all, as described by Captain Hinde in his "Fall of the Congo Arabs." Yet even in their case there are some points in the manner in which they deal with their aged—aged folks are not the most tempting eating—which shows some hint of survival from other times.

APPENDIX.

I.

ONE of the most scholarly and exhaustive books of recent years is certainly that of Mr. L. R. Farnell, Tutor of Merton College, Oxford, on the " Cults of the Greek States," published by the University Press. Mr. Farnell is not only an exact and thorough scholar, but a thinker. No point is overlooked, nor does he fail to follow up observances to what must have been their source or origin. The testimony of his great work from almost every point is in support of our position—that all significance of sacrifice there as elsewhere is due to its origin in human sacrifice—rather adverse, surely, to Professor Sayce's dictum that human sacrifice was practically unknown to the early Aryans, and

APPENDIX.

more especially to the Greeks. So strong is the evidence, and so completely is the impression strengthened by conclusions from every point, that Professor Sayce must, indeed, be suspected of speaking dogmatically of that which he had hardly studied and mastered as Mr. Farnell has. Just look at two points out of a *catena* that would fill such a little volume as ours :—

1.—" The title αἰγοφάγος, 'the goat-eater,' is found among the titles of Zeus, though we do not know the locality of the cult in which the name was in vogue; on the analogy of similar appellatives, we can certainly conclude that the name was derived from the actual cult, from some sacrificial ceremony, in which the god was supposed to partake of the flesh of one of his sacred animals,"[1] and this animal was so sacred because of presumed presence in it of the ancestral spirit or god.

2.—Speaking about the earlier worship of Artemis, Mr. Farnell has it :—

" This ritual, which seems very strange to us, but was quite natural from the totemistic

[1] "Cults of the Greek States," i. p. 96.

APPENDIX.

point of view, was certain to be misunderstood in the later period : *the mysterious sacrificial animal, which was treated as if it were man, was supposed to be treated thus, because it was a mere make-believe for the human offering which the goddess originally demanded.*[1]

Mr. Farnell finds, in fact, the "theanthropic animal" present universally in the Greek rites of sacrifice, and these facts unqualified can but point one way—to human sacrifice.

II.

"Talking of human sacrifices, Mr. Baring-Gould, in his just published 'Book of the West,' vol. ii., tells us that certain harvest customs, now dying out, such as the custom in Essex of catching a stranger in a twisted loop of straw, and holding him till he has paid a forfeit, or in Devon of 'making sweet hay,' are an almost certain proof that at a remote period our ancestors practised the awful rites at harvest and in spring, which are now found in use in Benin and other parts of Africa."[2]

[1] "Cults of the Greek States," ii. p. 441.
[2] "Literary World," Sept. 1, 1899.

APPENDIX.

III.

"A curious illustration of the universality of certain practices, which from their very nature might be supposed restricted in time and place, is afforded by the 'fire-dance' found flourishing in an aggravated form amongst the Catawbas [of South Carolina], as amongst the ancient Sabines, the Fijians, and so many other peoples. 'These miserable wretches are strangely infatuated with illness of the devil; it caused no small horror in me to see them . . . stand barefoot upon burning coal for nearly one hour, and then, recovering [? their] senses, leap out of fire without hurt or sign of any.'"[1]

---

[1] Lederer, quoted by James Mooney, "The Siouan Tribes of the East," Washington, 1894, p. 71.

INDEX.

Abel's and Cain's sacrifices, 11
Aben Ezra, quoted, 45
Abraham's offering of Isaac, 178—179
Adam of Bremen, quoted, 67
Aghoras, 83
Alus, sacrifice at, 65
Anglican orders, Pope's recognition of, 152
Antique customs, truly, 160
Arcadian Zeus, human sacrifice to, 65
"Athenæum, The," and surprising statements, 113
Atticottis, the, 123—124, 125
Australian human sacrifice, 121
Australian Yulugundis, 84
Aztecs, 132

Bain's principle, Professor, 146
Baring-Gould, Mr., 133
Battaks, 83
"Baw-dee-that-do," the Burman, 143
Bayin, Abd el, 101—103
Beth-els—God's houses, 3
Bethlehem, "house of bread," 21
Bleek, quoted, 189—190, 213
Bohlen, Von, 50, 193

INDEX

Borlase's "Dolmens of Ireland," 68, 126
Bread of mourners, 22
Buddha's body cut up, 131
Bunting, Mr. Percy W., 122
Burgess, Dr., 15
"Burma Census Report,' 91
Burrows, Captain Guy, on origin of cannibalism, 96
Burton, Sir Richard, 44, 46

CAIN's and Abel's sacrifices, 11
Cannibals, Captain Hinde on, 86; custom prevalent among advanced tribes, 87, 89, 90
Canterbury, Archbishop of, 153
Captivity, prior to, 175
Captivity, the, 214
Catawbas of Carolina, 219
Cæsar, quoted, 74—75
Caste, priesthoods promoters of, 164
Cecil, Lord Hugh, 158, 159, 160
Césaréda caves, 69
Chalmers, Mr., New Guinea, 128
Cicero on eating gods, 117
Circumcision, 179
Children sacrificed in Greece, 65
Chinese festival—survival of human sacrifice in, 112
Chinese, human sacrifice among, 113
Church of England, not reformed, 158
Clytemnestra, dromos of, 72
Colenso, 170, 213
Commentators hard put to it about *corban* and *zebach*, 1
Confucian and Taouist temples, 132
Congo cannibals, 215
Corn-god, the, 118

INDEX.

"Cornhill Magazine, The," 156
Creation, priest in sacrificing imitates act of, 18
Creighton, Dr. Mandell, with taste will make reply, 43
Cross symbol and Mayas, 133; and Yucatan, 133
Cucumas of South America, 85
Cut up an animal, sacrifice to, 17

"DAILY CHRONICLE, The," quoted, 157
Dalton, quoted, 82
Daniel, the prophet, 117, 118
David and Rizpah, 134; David and Joshua, 135
David, "full flower of Hebrew monotheism," 186
Dead, laws against mourning for the, 19
Delgado, Mr., 69
De Quincey and sacrificial feasting, 25
Deuteronomic law, the, 190
Diipolia and rites, 41
Dionysius of Halicarnassus, 28
Dionysos, fawn sacred to, and skin worn by his priests, 52
Dobson, Mr. George, 108, 109
Dods, Dr. Marcus, 184
Druids, Keltic, human sacrifices, 61, 74
Druids, the, and skin of sacrifice, 51
Duncker, quoted, 85
Dyaks of Borneo, 111

EALES, Mr., and Burma customs, 91
"Eaten with honour," 122—123
Eating from hatred, 83
Eating with the god—sacrifice, 5
Easter, the full moon of, 134
Edkins, Dr., Chinese missionary, 132
Eggeling, Dr., quoted, 61, 64, 161

INDEX.

Egyptians and Libyans, and human sacrifice, 123
Elijah, 208
Emerson, quoted, 4
Encounter Bay, people of, 145
Ewerbeck, 50
Ezekiel, 172, 195, 196
Ezekiel and his denunciations, 19

FAIRBAIRN, Principal's, ingenuity, his "akin to the Divine," 26, 27, 28, 148
Farnell, Mr., and the Greek rites, 41, 55, 65, 218—218
Father Earth, 138
Fenton, Captain, on eating elderly relations, 91
Fertit tribe, the, 101
First idea of sacrifice, sharing with ancestors, 6
Flamen Dialis, the, 118
Flesh identified with soul in sacrifice, 5
Food and nourishment always associated with *berith*, 18
" Food of men," 19
Food, human, agreeable to the gods, 3
Frazer, Mr., and "Golden Bough," 140
Freeman, Dr., quoted, 155
Freemasonry, 156
Free-thought, 156

GAHMAN, Mek, of Senaar, 103
Ganesa, Hindu, 50
Geddes, Dr., and Magee, 16
Ghillany, 50, 193, 193—4
Gifoon, Ali Effendi, 101
Gift, all words for sacrifice in Hebrew mean, 14
Gill, Dr. Wyatt, and Mangaian human sacrifice, 127
Gill, Dr. Wyatt, and the heavenly race, 145

INDEX.

Gladstone, W. E., 163, 164
Gladstone's promised book on Pope and Ang orders, 162
God-eating, indirect, very common, 77
God-eating, second step in process, 4
God invited to eat share of sacrifice, 4
God, sacrificing priest identified with, 50
God's vineyard, the gates of, 159
"Golden Bough," and Mr. Frazer, 140
Golden calf, Hebrews drank it, 144
Gould, Mr. Baring-, 133
Granger, Dr. F., 183
Greece, children sacrificed in, 65
Greeks and human sacrifice, 114
Greeks, the, and skin of sacrifice, 57
Gregory the Second, 68
Grimm on sacrifice, 3
Grinnell, George Bird, and Pawnees, 137—138
Guatemala, in, 99

HALIFAX, Lord, 93, 161, 162
Halked, quoted, 63
Hanifa tribe of Arabs and lump of dough, 48
Hartland's "Perseus," quoted, 141 (and note
Hatred, eating from, 83
Hayti, Indian of, 98
Head, why was it never eaten? 30
Heathen Semites, 79
Hebrews and the dead, the early, 135
Hebrews and skin of burnt offering, 56; the pries had it, and why? 57
Hebrew *Rephaim*, 146; many meanings of root word,
Hercules abolished human sacrifices, 39

INDEX.

Hewitt, Mr., and high places, 160 (note)
Hillier and skins worn by Bantus, 57
Hinde, Captain, on cannibals, 86
Hinde, Captain, quoted, 215
Hindu feasts to the dead, 24
Hoama and Soma drink, 150
Hommel, F., not Homme, 114
Horse-sacrifice, 114
Hosea, with characteristic verse, 42, 43
Human flesh forbidden to women, 97; if *hunger* motive, why so? 97
Human sacrifice, all sacrifice a substitution for, 31—35
Human sacrifice among Hebrews, 147
Human sacrifices and early Irish, 61; and early Welsh, 61
Hunger motive, if, why is human flesh forbidden to women? 97
Hupfeld, quoted, 148
Huysman's words, 156

INCENSE, 9
Irish and human sacrifices, the early, 61
Isaac, Abraham's offering of, 177—179; why so linked with Passover, 180
Isaiah, 205

JAHWÉ and his eatings, 22, 25, 28
Jehu, 209
Jephthah, 149
Jeremiah, 172, 191
Jessopp, Dr., and clerical freeholds, 165
Jezebels, painted, 154

INDEX.

Jordan, beyond, 173, 174
Joshua at Ai, 134; Joshua and David, 135
KHOND sacrifice, the, 78, 125, 131
Khonds, 183
Khonds of Orissa, 99, 105—106, 108, 109, 112, 215
Kidneys, seat of life, 85
Kuenen, 135

LANG, Mr. A., 199, 204
Lang, Mr. A., and god-eating, 46, 113, 139—140
Laphystius cult, 41
Laws against mourning for the dead, 19
Lectisternia, heathen, 20
Levi, rod of, which swallowed up all other rods, 55
Levites, the, 187, 191
Levitical ordinances, 74
Libyans and Egyptians, and human sacrifice, 121
Livingstone and the Manyemas, 94
Long barrows of Yorkshire, 68
Lubbock, Sir John, 81; sacrificial victim regarded as the god, 81; on the New Zealander, 92, 142
Lupercal, at the, 73
Lustration, rite of, 23
Lycæan Zeus, worship of, 73
Lycæum, sacrifice on Mount, 65

MACKAY, quoted, 212
McArthur's Church Discipline Bill, 159
MacDonald, A., 84
Macpherson, Major, and the Khonds, 125
Magee, Dr. William, on *minchah*, 9, 14, 70
Mahommed's reform abolishing priesthood, 36
Maine, Sir Henry, misleading, 114
Manatt, Dr., 71

INDEX.

Mangaia and human sacrifice, 126
Manna, food of the mighty, 11
Marshall, Captain, and Gifoon, 101
Master, Lieutenant, 91
Mayas and cross symbol, 132
Meriah sacrifice, the, 107, 108, 137, 185
Meriah sacrifices, 215
Mexicans, sacrificer's masks, 50
Minchah, meaning of the, 6—9; a gift, 7; a cake, 9; derivation is *corban*, not *zebach*, 12, 13, 49
Moab, king of, and human sacrifice, 115
Moloch, 203
Moloch and bull worship, 44; Moloch found with an ox's head, 44
Mommsen, quoted, 162
Morley, Mr. John, 163
Mosaic economy carries forward big substitutionary scheme, 46
Mosaic legislation, 76
Moses and golden calf, 144
Mother Corn, 138
Mourning for dead, laws against, 19
Mycenæans, the, 71

NESFIELD'S, Mr., caste system, 23
New Guinea, human sacrifice in, 96, 128
New Zealanders, 100
Newcome, Old, quoted, 45
Niger coast, people of the, 109
Northmen, early, and human sacrifice, 74

OANNES and split fish as robe, 52
Oath takings on skin or head of sacrificial animal, 53

INDEX.

Ocaisir, the Arabian, 35
Œdipus the king, 66
" Old and tough," not young and tender, 122
Oorigas of Burma, the, and human sacrifice, 125
Oort's demonstration, 134
Osiris, body of, cut up in parts, 131
"Ox" in Bible is wrong, Hebrews did not castrate cattle, 44

PASCAL lamb, 34
Passover of the Hebrews, 169, 187—188, 211
Papuans of the Solomon Islands, 94
Paul, Mr. C. Kegan, 155, 156
Pawnee Indians and their religion, 138—139
Pawnees, the, and human sacrifice, 127
Pennu, Tarri, the Khond earth-goddess, 125
Perowne, Dr. J. J. S., 201, 202
Perowne's, Dr., words, 147
Pesach, the, 170, 176
Petrie, Professor Flinders, 119, 120—123
Phallus, the, carried, 79
Philistines, 179
Phylarchus, as quoted by Porphyry, 64
Pliny, quoted, 70
Plumptre, Dean, 66
Pope of Rome, 165, 166
Potraj festival, 23, 38
Pragâpati, 33
Priest in sacrificing imitates act of creation, 18
Priesthoods, promoters of caste, 164
Priestley, referred to, 15
Purana, Calica, 183
Purushamedha, human sacrifice, 63

INDEX.

Purusha-pasu, human sacrificial victim, 63

REAL presence, the, 151
Rigveda, 163
Rigveda, priest sacrifice as well as sacrificer in the, 58, 61
Rivers, sacred, 80
Rizpah watching, 134
Rods with the Hebrews, 55
Romans and human sacrifices, 115; and eating of beans, 116
Roman Mars, the, 142
Roth, Mr. H. Ling, 111

SACRAMENT, unholy, 93
Sacred rivers, 80
Sacrifice, all words for, in Hebrew, mean gift, 14
Sacrifice, eating with the god, 3; first idea sharing food with ancestors, 6
Sacrifice, god-eating, 77
Sacrifice, parts of, used to bless the fields, 37
" Sacrificers of men," kissing calves, 43
Sacrificing priests identified with god, 50
St. Jerome and the Atticottis, 123
St. Matthew's, Westminster, 157
Sāktas and Tantrikas, 98
Sanskrit has word for human sacrifice, as one division of sacrifices, 61; it has term "purusha-pasu," man as sacrificial victim, 63; how did they get into that language, Professor Sayce? 61; human sacrifice in, 114
Satapatha Brâhmana, quoted, 32, 33, 42, 61, 63
Saul's crime, 134

INDEX.

Sayce, Professor, 17 ; and human sacrifice in Rigveda, 59, 60, 62, 64, 66—67
Schliemann, Dr., 71
Scott, Mr. J. G., on Burma, 143
Scythians, the, 105
Sem priests in Egypt and skin of panther, 53
Semites, heathen, 79
Sharpe, Mr. S., 192
Sheol, 136
Shewbread, table of, 20
Shin-wei or Ling-wei, 132
Sin-offering of the Hebrews, 33
Siva, and his forms, 49 ; highest sacrificing priest, 49
Smith, Professor Robertson, 34, 41, 107
South Pacific, tribes of, 100
" Spectator, The," quoted, 175
Spencer, Mr. Herbert, 180
Sphinx, the, 66—67
Spirits of the unburied, 136
Star-worshippers' sacrifice, 48, 49
Strabo, 75
Stupas, Hindu, their origin, 131
Substitution universal, 37
Substitutionary process seen almost everywhere else, 47
Sun-sign, the, 133
Swedes, human sacrifice among the, 67
Sykes referred to, 15, 49

TANTRIKAS and Sāktas, 98
Tarri Pennu, 78, 100, 125
Tarianas and Tulchas of Brazil, 82
Taouist and Confucian temples, 132
Teoqualo, the Mexican, 142

INDEX.

Tezcatlipoca, yearly sacrifice of, 142—143
Thor, hammer of, 133
Theanthropic animal, the, 30
Theologians, learned, close their eyes, 15
Toltecs, 132
Totem-beast, the, 141
Train's "Isle of Man," 209
Trepanning, posthumous, 69—70
Tupinambas of Brazil, 98, 107
Tuscaroras, the, 145
Tylor, Dr. E. B., quoted on Mexico, 141

UNHOLY sacrament, 93
Upsal, awful grove of, 67

VEDIC sacrifices, all feedings of gods, 24
Venables, Canon, quoted, 204
Venezuelans, 83
Victim, the sacrificial, regarded as the god, 81
Villaneuva, 123
Von Bohlen, 50, 193

WAFER, the Roman, 39; wafers instituted by Numa Pompilius, 40; Roman Catholic wafer a mere copy, 39
Washing of priests, 28; among Navajo and Zuni Indians, 29
Ward, Herbert, on cannibals, 88
Wellhausen, 135
Welsh, early, and human sacrifices, 61
Women, if hunger motive, why is human flesh forbidden to, 97
Wool and milk, &c., 13; difficulties of commentators here, 13, 14

INDEX.

Worsaae, quoted, 69
Wright, Professor Theodore, quoted, 92

XOMANES of Mexico, 82

YAMAS of South America, 85
York, Archbishop of, 153
Yorkshire, long barrows of, 68
Yucatan, cross symbol, 132
Yulugundis of Australia, 84

ZEUS, human sacrifice to the Arcadian, 65
Zeus, Lycæan, in Arcadia, 73
Zobeir Pasha, 101
Zuni Indians, 133 (note)
Zwemer, Rev. Samuel M., and star-worshippers' sacrifice, 48

THE END.

www.ingramcontent.com/pod-product-compliance
Lightning Source LLC
Chambersburg PA
CBHW031746230426

43669CB00007B/507